God Saves

God Saves

Rethinking Christianity's
Most Controversial Doctrine—
and Why It Matters

Wayne G. Boulton

FOREWORD BY
Matthew Myer Boulton

CASCADE *Books* · Eugene, Oregon

GOD SAVES
Rethinking Christianity's Most Controversial Doctrine—and Why It Matters

Cascade Books
An Imprint of Wipf and Stock Publishers
199 W. 8th Ave., Suite 3
Eugene, OR 97401

www.wipfandstock.com

PAPERBACK ISBN: 978-1-7252-9212-3
HARDCOVER ISBN: 978-1-7252-9213-0
EBOOK ISBN: 978-1-7252-9214-7

Cataloguing-in-Publication data:

Names: Boulton, Wayne G., author. | Boulton, Matthew Myer, foreword.

Title: God saves : rethinking Christianity's most controversial doctrine—and why it matters / by Wayne G. Boulton ; foreword by Matthew Myer Boulton.

Description: Eugene, OR: Cascade Books, 2022 | Includes bibliographical references and index.

Identifiers: ISBN 978-1-7252-9212-3 (paperback) | ISBN 978-1-7252-9213-0 (hardcover) | ISBN 978-1-7252-9214-7 (ebook)

Subjects: LCSH: Election (Theology). | Reformed Church—Doctrines—History.

Classification: BT810 .B69 2022 (print) | BT810 (ebook)

01/12/22

For Vicki,
my beloved helpmeet
of fifty-two years

Foreword

THIS BOOK TOOK SHAPE over the last ten years of my father's life, and most intensively during the last two, as he lived with pancreatic cancer. We met weekly during the latter period to discuss drafts and debate details, a father and son wrestling over theology—as we had by then for more than three decades. My career turned toward theology in no small part because of those good-humored wrestling matches. And here was Dad, absorbed in one last book project, searching and researching, writing and rewriting, as he walked through the valley of the shadow of death, always with a twinkle in his eye. The book's subject, appropriately enough, was destiny: the doctrine of predestination, or, as it is sometimes called, the doctrine of election.

Destiny has always struck me as a quintessentially American fascination. On one hand, the country's defining myths are often entangled with claims of "manifest destiny," a phrase used both by nineteenth-century imperialists to justify westward expansion and by Frederick Douglass to describe the anti-slavery cause of the Civil War. Variations on the theme appear as far back as 1630, in John Winthrop's "City on a Hill" sermon, and as recently as the pop-culture juggernauts du jour, from *Star Wars* to *The Matrix* to Harry Potter and on and on. From this angle, destiny is a leitmotif at the heart of American culture, rhetoric, and mythology. But on the other hand, at the same time, the very idea of "destiny"—that is, of a preset pathway and outcome for a person's life and work—would seem to directly contradict that other celebrated American myth, the capacity to be "self-made," to be "free" from constraints, to blaze one's own trail and fashion one's own future. Westerners generally, and Americans in particular, are often at pains to claim freedom from a wide range of would-be determinisms: biological, familial, behavioral, economic, and sociopolitical. "Don't tread on me," read one iconic flag of the American Revolution. And yet we still thrill to the idea of destiny, of traveling a path prepared in advance. Both Calvinist and Roman Catholic communities took root in that same revolutionary American soil, and both John Calvin and Thomas Aquinas wrote plainly and powerfully of "predestination."

This basic, apparent contradiction, woven as it is into the DNA of the American experience, may help explain why, over time, the doctrine of predestination has fallen out of favor—or indeed out of sight—in many Christian communities today. The teaching was always controversial, of course, but its defenders are increasingly difficult to find, even among the descendants of Calvin and Aquinas. Why? Not least, one imagines, because for some, the doctrine seems to contradict prized ideals of individual liberty, agency, and control. Or similarly, for others, the idea that a person's path and destination are preset may lead too easily to complacency, fatalism, or decadence. And moreover, as Dad persuasively argues in this volume, since any doctrine of "election" implies an "elect" group singled out for special divine favor, the teaching may well come across as three repellent things at once: a classic case of religious hubris; an occasion for anxious obsession over whether one is "in" or "out"; and, most devastating of all, a divisive carving-up of the world into the saved and the damned.

But all this is precisely why, the more I talked with Dad about this book project, the more convinced I became that he was on to something. It's not just that the criticisms just outlined misunderstand the doctrine of election in various ways; it's that they actively distort and invert the teaching's potential advantages into liabilities, beating plowshares into swords. Indeed, on closer inspection, at its best, the doctrine of election is a humbling teaching, not a hubristic one; an assuring teaching, not a disquieting one; and above all, a reconciling teaching, not a divisive one. To put Dad's thesis most sharply, the Christian tradition knows only too well that religious doctrine can be hubristic, disquieting, and divisive—and so our ancestors set out to build doctrinal guardrails against these dangers, and one such guardrail became known as "the doctrine of predestination" or "the doctrine of election." The fact that this guardrail itself is now routinely understood as a cause of the very perils it's meant to protect us from is a case study in how ideas can become misconstrued—but more importantly, it's also a clear sign that the doctrine itself requires recovery and renovation for the twenty-first century. If this book contributes to that larger goal, I know Dad would be delighted.

I hasten to add, however, that to speak of "the Christian tradition" and "our ancestors" and "guardrails" in this way is by no means to endorse everything Calvin or Aquinas or anyone else taught about predestination; indeed, the teaching's questionable reputation today has had as much to do with its advocates as with its critics. Rather, to appeal generally to "tradition" or "ancestry" is precisely to stand at an intentional distance from any particular treatise or individual, the better to discern a kind of collective intellectual lineage through time, descending from Genesis, Exodus, and the prophets, through Jesus and Paul and the theologians who followed, and ultimately down to our own day. By taking this long view, we may better make out what the doctrine of election means for us today; we may hear, so to speak, what "the tradition" is trying to say to us here and now. In some respects, the message we discern may comport closely with what Calvin or Aquinas argued, but in other respects, it may not. For example, as I have argued elsewhere, Calvin too often violates his own well-reasoned rules against speculating about who is or isn't included among the elect, the size of the overall group, and so on—an inconsistency that regrettably laid groundwork for the clannish forms the doctrine has sometimes taken among his "Calvinist" descendants.[1] Learning from such mistakes, even as we embrace the best of what Calvin and others taught about predestination, is what it means to give "the tradition" a sympathetic, critical hearing, with an eye toward building a sound, life-giving doctrine of election for a new day.

Exactly how a teaching with a reputation for being arrogant, distressing, and divisive is actually a resource for humility, assurance, and companionship is the burden of this book's provocative argument. But there's yet another potential benefit of a renewed doctrine of election, one Dad touches on here and there, that may shed light on the distinctively American tension between "destiny" and "freedom," and ultimately on what human freedom is in the first place. Thinking through the doctrine of election evokes a picture of human freedom as a phenomenon deeply, inseparably, even symbiotically related to divine freedom: we may and do choose the good, and are free to do so, precisely insofar as God acts in us and through us—or, as Paul puts it, precisely insofar as "the Spirit of God dwells in you" (Rom 8:9). This indwelling is already a sign that God has elected a human being, has gracefully chosen her in love and mercy, and so has set out a destiny for her to freely follow in, with, and through God. Once genuine

---

1. See Boulton, *Life in God*, 138–65.

human life is understood in this way as intimate, ongoing symbiosis with God, as living-together-in-concert, the supposed contradiction between "destiny" and "freedom" falls away. On one hand, human freedom is revealed to be a creaturely liberty made possible by God's creative, constitutive, indwelling accompaniment. From this point of view, whether we are consciously aware of it or not, we cannot be free without God, but rather only with God—for God is, as Paul puts it in Athens, the One in whom "we live, and move, and have our being" (Acts 17:28). And on the other hand, accordingly, human destiny is revealed to be that path of life along which God prompts us and calls us, from within and from without. Far from denying or diminishing human freedom, then, the doctrine of predestination may help us understand that freedom in its fullest, highest form. And likewise, far from leading to complacency or passivity, the doctrine may encourage us to humbly, boldly, continuously act, for "the Spirit of God dwells in you"—and God, after all, is on a mission.

An analogy from music might be clarifying. When a composer writes a symphony, it doesn't occur to us to think that she has imposed something on the symphony, restricting or confining it in some way—for the symphony does not already exist apart from her, as a separate thing over against which she may or may not impose her will. Rather, the symphony exists in the first place as an expression of her will, her artistry, her genius. For the first violin section, she has set out a pathway as a part of the overall work, now harmonizing, now dissonant, now carrying the primary theme, now receding into the background. She has done so in advance, of course, as part of the musical score—and here again, it doesn't occur to us to conceive the composer's work as somehow restrictive for the first violin section, but rather the opposite: we conceive it as empowering, as creative, as something the composer is giving the first violin section as an avenue of participation and contribution to the symphony. Now, perhaps the most fundamental of all Christian ideas is that God is the composer, we might say, of the symphony of creation. Accordingly, the notion that a person stands separate and over against God such that she may be constrained or coerced by divine election, rather than liberated and empowered by it, is a kind of category mistake. For in fact, insofar as she stands, she stands not over against God but with God, in God, and by the grace of God in the first place. Understood from this angle, the doctrine of election is no lure toward fatalistic complacency, but rather a provocation to pick up our instrument and play.

The German-American theologian Paul Tillich makes a similar point from a different angle, drawing a threefold distinction between autonomy, or self-governance; heteronomy, or being governed by an "other"; and theonomy, or divine governance, which for Tillich is the deepest, most comprehensive reality of the three.[2] Precisely because God is at once the maker of our being, the giver of all good gifts in our lives, and an abiding, indwelling presence all the way along, divine commands come to us not only from an "other" outside of us, but also from within. After all, God is the one—as in the composer analogy—who creatively bestows the basic form or "law" of our creaturely being; and at the same time, God is the one in whom we live, and move, and have our being, who indwells us, and whom we, in turn, indwell: "Abide in me, as I abide in you" (John 15:4). In this sense, every divine command is a blend of both heteronomy and autonomy. God urges and exhorts us both down from without and up from within.

Tillich primarily applies this idea to the sphere of ethics, but a similar insight may shed light on the supposed contradiction between "freedom" and "destiny." Think of it this way: it's only if we conceive—or rather, misconceive—destiny as strictly heteronomous, as an imposition or gravitational force emanating from outside of us, that we may think of it as though it is in conflict with autonomy or "freedom." But if instead we conceive destiny as theonomous, as divine governance that comes to us both from without and from within, the supposed opposition dissolves. To the extent that we live out our destiny, we simultaneously follow God's call and our own most deeply held, most authentic desires—for those desires are themselves ongoing divine gifts. From this point of view, destiny and freedom are two sides of the same coin: we are free, we might say, precisely insofar as we live out, with God's graceful help, the destiny God gives us. Moreover, if the idea of theonomy helps illuminate human destiny and freedom, it may well point the way toward a theonomous understanding of human being itself.

In the end, then, careful clarification of the doctrine of election of the sort found in this book may open up a range of avenues for further research and development, including a broad reappraisal of how best to understand human life, divine life, and human life together with God. But first, Dad contends, to grapple with the doctrine, we must grapple with Paul's letter to the church in Rome; and to understand that letter, we must grapple with the ancient sources on which Paul drew to make his case:

2. See Tillich, *Systematic Theology*, 83; and "Moralisms," 135.

the admonitions of the prophets, the freedom of the exodus from Egypt, the escapades of the patriarchs and matriarchs, and the contours of the creation in Genesis. For his part, Dad drew on his whole life and career to build this book, his years as an ethics professor and theological school president, to be sure, and even more, his years as a pastor. And by the end of it all, he was convinced that two words—God saves—lay at the heart of human experience, and that to understand them well is a life's work, a life well spent, a good-humored wrestling match to leaven and enliven our days, always with a twinkle in our eyes.

Matthew Myer Boulton

Thanksgiving, 2021
Keene, New Hampshire

Acknowledgments

I'VE READ A LOT of books. On the cover of them all, including this one, is a myth: the author's solitary name. Writers know better. Every single book, one way or another, is a team effort.

Let me begin with two rabbis who have helped me a great deal. The first, Rabbi Brett Krichiver, is leading a historic Reform synagogue—Indianapolis Hebrew Congregation—to new heights as God's beloved and chosen ones. The second is Orthodox Rabbi Irving Greenberg, whose influential career has long endeavored to overcome the hostility between Judaism and Christianity. While never ceasing to be a Jew, Greenberg grasps the Christian faith in bold, capacious ways that both stun and inspire me, a lifelong Christian.

The work of Fleming Rutledge, an Episcopal priest and preacher of singular gifts, has been indispensable along the way. Rutledge's ministry and writing are a sustained attack on the neglect, and even the disparagement, of the Old Testament in many Christian communities today. If we lose the Old Testament, we lose the doctrine of election, for those Hebrew Scriptures—no less than the first nine-tenths of the Bible!—are the raw material from which that doctrine is drawn, not least by Paul in Romans 8–12. Peter Thuesen, the author of *Predestination*, arguably the finest short history of the doctrine of election ever written, has become a trusted advisor and friend. Likewise, at Western Seminary in Holland, Michigan, Suzanne McDonald—an Australian election scholar—is a spirited comrade and colleague with a fine feel for the importance of writing for the church. And on the subject of Christian doctrine itself, the lucid and adventurous work of Luther scholar and religious studies professor Christine Helmer came to my attention just in time.

Much like organisms with genetic code, Reformed and Presbyterian institutions carry election doctrines forward from generation to generation, and I stand today in debt to a number of them. At Lafayette College in Pennsylvania, I was given the opportunity to participate in a student-run "College Church," as well as to organize a campus-wide study of a 1952 inspirational classic that just happened to have election nestled inside it: *Your God is Too Small*, by J. B. Phillips. At Hope Park Church in St. Andrews, Scotland, my family and I were shaped and formed by the bracing, generous Church of Scotland ministry of Reverend William Henney, his wife Margaret, and their delightful family. At Hope College in Michigan, a school associated with the Reformed Church in America, any lingering doubts I may have had about whether the Reformed tradition could exist and even flourish outside my own Presbyterian Church were soon forgotten.

The imprint of my Chicago seminary—McCormick Theological Seminary (PCUSA)—is difficult to overstate. While there, I gained the courage to see myself suited for a public role in Christian service. An unforgettable first assignment came my way at McCormick as a missionary (or "Frontier Intern," as we then were called) on the other side of the globe in Thailand, from 1967 to 1969. Using the language of the church, I was "elected" to this role and, within that election, experienced a "call." Over the decades that followed, seven of us who first met as students at McCormick in the 1960s have gathered annually, flying in from states as far-flung as Arizona, Minnesota, Massachusetts, and Texas. "The Dogs," we call ourselves, and the name fits. The Reverends Don Dempsey, Dale Hartwig, Steve Shoemaker, Gordon Stewart, Harry Strong, and Bob Young have built up treasures in heaven by doing penitential work on earth—that is, they have read parts of this book in draft form, and graciously have helped me strengthen them. These are the kind of conversation partners most authors only dream about.

I find myself dangerously proud of my most recent home church, the ecclesial setting within which my thinking about the doctrine of election came to fruition: Second Presbyterian Church in Indianapolis. Reverend Lewis Galloway, Second's former senior pastor, now retired, is certainly one of the finest and somehow also one of the funniest leaders in the Presbyterian Church (USA). His talented successor, Reverend Christopher Henry, is fast becoming one of the brightest lights in the church's national leadership; my new friendship with him has been a great blessing. The Theologian in Residence at Second Church, Dr. John Franke, has become that rare presence in anyone's life: a spiritual conversation partner. His assistance in improving this manuscript and moving it toward publication has been invaluable. Moreover, out of Second Church and nearby Presbyterian churches have come many others: Tom Bast, Bob Hunter, Carol Johnston, RuthAnn and Don McPherson, Elyssa and Jim Montgomery, Sue and Norm Myer, and Harriet Wilkins.

On the near north side of Indianapolis is the campus of Christian Theological Seminary, an ecumenical school of the Christian Church (Disciples of Christ). The premiere Protestant seminary in the city, CTS has helped me in countless ways—not the least of which has been its library, recently under the leadership of Dr. Anthony Elia, who welcomed me with open arms as the research for this book took shape. Reverend Dr. Allan Boesak, during his time as visiting professor at CTS, helped me see clearly what I now firmly believe: that election is to be grasped as a prophetic doctrine from start to finish.

I turn, finally, to my own family. My older son, Matt, has been an irreplaceable theological conversation partner since, oh, age fifteen; I dare say the Apostle Paul's reflections on diversity, truth-telling, and unity in Ephesians 4 illumine the relationship. I am grateful to him for helping to edit and shepherd this book to publication. My younger son, Christopher, lifts my life in innumerable ways, including helping me to see how the doctrine of election, as he once put it, "saves us from ourselves." This leaves only my wife, Vicki, to whom God has guided me and for whom the words of the book's dedication will have to do, insufficient as they are. Of Jewish heritage herself (though now a good Presbyterian), her formative impact on me, and on this book, goes well beyond my capacity to describe.

Introduction

Election is not a Reformed doctrine. It is a doctrine for the whole church. For all the problems raised by the use of particular formulations, and for all the debate surrounding the various ways of understanding it, the concept of election itself lies at the very heart of the scriptural narrative of God's dealings with the world. —Suzanne McDonald[1]

MOST OF MY LIFE, I've been a teacher. So it is a joy to write a book like this one: a teaching book about a particular teaching. The term *doctrine* means a religious teaching or instruction, and the doctrine I have in mind is one of Christianity's most ancient ideas—older than Christianity itself, in fact. It is also one of its most controversial, even to the point of being opposed, suppressed, diminished, ignored, or forgotten by many Christians today. In some circles, it's called the doctrine of election; in others, the doctrine of predestination. Over the centuries, it has become arguably the most unpopular Christian doctrine of all, both inside and outside the church—and the reasons why are not hard to find.

For one, the doctrine is often understood to be primarily about a special group, "the elect," "the chosen," those God has decided to save—and as such, it seems to be the epitome of religious pride. Second, the doctrine is often understood to create anxiety about whether or not a given person or a loved one is in this special group—and if there's one thing our world needs less of, it's religious anxiety. Third and most damningly, the doctrine is often understood as divisive, carving up the world into two camps. In a world that desperately needs reconciliation and community,

1. McDonald, *Re-Imaging Election*, xiv–xv.

the doctrine of election can seem intent on dividing sheep from goats, elect from reprobate, found from lost, good Christians from bad Christians—and indeed good Christians from everybody else, including members of other religions or no religion at all.

These are powerful, compelling objections. No wonder the doctrine is so often deemed to be a source of pride, anxiety, and division. No wonder so many Christians oppose it, distance themselves from it, ignore it, or have simply set it aside, hoping it fades away.

And yet: in this book I argue that the doctrine of election is an indispensable source of life and wisdom for the church, and for individual Christians. The doctrine's critics, I contend, have radically misunderstood it—often with considerable assistance from its supposed defenders! That is, rightly grasped, the doctrine of election is a profound source of Christian humility, not pride; assurance, not anxiety; and companionship, not division, even and especially when it comes to interreligious relations. In other words, predestination's conventional reputation today is a perfect reversal of its genuine purpose and potential in human life. Reclaiming this purpose and potential, and thereby rediscovering why the doctrine at its best has been so foundational to Christian thought for millennia, is my aim in these pages.

The doctrine of election is not explicit in the earliest ecumenical creeds of the church, and even today, parts of the Christian community do not assent to it. Augustine of Hippo in the fifth century, Thomas Aquinas in the thirteenth, John Calvin in the sixteenth, and many others have explicitly embraced and defended the idea, while John Wesley and his Methodists, for example, did the contrary. Upon arriving with the Pilgrims on American soil, the Reformed doctrinal complex known as "predestination"—along with furious and sustained arguments against it—spread like a prairie fire across the landscape for 400 years, involving Catholics as well as Protestants, Lutherans as well as Baptists.[2] The smoking embers lie all around us.[3]

Despite the controversy it stirs, however, and in some ways because of it, election is a Christian doctrine of enormous and continuing spiritual

2. Though I will use the terms *election* and *predestination* interchangeably in this book, I will most often use the former term, both for the sake of simplicity and because the latter term is so frequently associated with alleged divine arbitrariness and determinism (each being a profound misreading of the doctrine).

3. For a brilliant overview of the doctrine's history in the American context, see Peter Thuesen's *Predestination*.

power. At its best, it is foundational for the faith, near the root of all that Jesus taught, said, and did—though in the Gospels, he characteristically speaks implicitly *from* the doctrine and hardly ever explicitly *about* it. Even the rare stories containing conspicuous divine election language (for example, Jesus' baptism and transfiguration) use the framework of Mt. Sinai and its cloud, suggesting a great mystery as well as a clear message. In Paul's writing, and in particular in his Letter to the Romans, the argument is more overt and expository. And both in Paul and in the Gospels, we find the doctrine articulated in ways that draw deeply on the wellsprings found in that ancient library Christians call the Old Testament.

But even if we find the idea of election attested variously throughout Scripture, we may ask: How on earth could the notion of being "elected" or "chosen" by God give rise to humility? The key here is to see how the teaching's intended impact is to engender modesty and reserve about one's own faith, and indeed, about all faith and religion *per se*. Properly conceived, the doctrine is an attack on religious pride, not an occasion for it. The teaching's force is to expose the corrupting arrogance too often generated by religious doctrine itself, its capacity to create a sense of possessing a truth and therefore gaining an advantage. The doctrine of election, in brief, is the doctrine that doctrine will not save us. Religion will not save us. Good behavior will not save us. God does all the saving, and God decides to do so quite apart from doctrine, religion, and human behavior. This is also the source of the doctrine's profound assurance, its counter to religious anxiety, since it insists in the strongest possible terms that our hope is in God, not in religious doctrines or devout practices or excellent works. Doctrines, practices, and works can be extremely valuable, of course—but they do not save. Only God can do that. And because God does do that, because God saves, we can rightly and assuredly place our hope and conviction not in ourselves but in God: that God will save us, our loved ones, and the world besides. Rightly grasped, the doctrine of election means that in each and every individual case, our own and our neighbor's, we cannot rule out the possibility that God will save, or that God is already at work doing so. Since saving is God's business, not ours, we cannot definitively declare universal salvation—but we can and should pray for it, and hope for it, and even dare, in faith and love, to expect it.

This good news, properly received, not only releases us from anxiety—it also releases us into genuine freedom, for God and for others. Precisely because it declares that religions do not save, and that our destinies are already determined "before," so to speak, all our intellectual and moral and spiritual work, the doctrine of election opens the door to living life as a discernment of a destiny, an answer to a call, and a communion with God woven into a fabric that includes the manifold destinies and callings of others. If our role is to save ourselves, then life becomes a relentless jockeying for divine favor, and a manic attempt to convince others to save themselves, too; but if God saves, the question of divine favor is already settled, and our relationships with others may unfold with an equanimity that makes genuine love and respect possible. This includes relationships with fellow Christians, of course, but also with Jews, Muslims, Hindus, and neighbors from other religions and no religion at all. The doctrine of election teaches that God's love for us both includes and transcends our religious affiliations, or lack thereof. In other words, if religions do not save, we dare not draw an apparent "circle of the saved" along religious lines.

An important instance of this understanding of the doctrine is the relationship between Christianity and Judaism—a crucial matter in its own right, and also a kind of case study within Paul's Letter to the Romans, exemplifying the doctrine's power as a source of authentic, healthy community. When the Second Vatican Council of the Roman Catholic Church struggled with just this issue in the 1960s, Jaroslav Pelikan wrote that the Council's conclusion was the most forceful church statement on the subject in almost two millennia, "at least since the ninth, tenth, and eleventh chapters of the Epistle to the Romans, upon which it was based."[4] The Council overturned centuries of Christian anti-Judaism—and it did so not despite its understanding of election, but precisely because of it. In the pages that follow, I build on Vatican II's move toward reconciliation, but in a Protestant key, demonstrating how the doctrine of election opens the door to new levels of healthy companionship between Christians and Jews, and by extension, between Christians and countless others as well.

Thus the doctrine of election or predestination, so far from its widespread reputation as a source of pride, anxiety, and division, is actually—rightly grasped—one of the church's most precious sources of humility, assurance, and companionship. Mistaken interpretations of it abound, of course, but that is no reason to cut ourselves off from the depth of its riches. Indeed, the most common mistake about election is one to which my own Presbyterian and Reformed tradition is both vulnerable

4. Pelikan, *The Christian Tradition, Vol. 5*, 334. As we shall see, Romans 8 and 12 are indispensable as well.

and particularly sensitive: namely, to approach the teaching as if it is primarily about "the elect." On the contrary, at its core, the teaching is actually about God, and what it proclaims is the radiant good news that God saves. This is the Christian gospel in two words: *God saves*. We don't. Good behavior doesn't. Religion doesn't. Doctrine doesn't. Only God. Or, if you prefer the gospel in one word: *Jesus*—a Greek transliteration from the Hebrew *Yeshua*, meaning "God saves."

Finally, while overturning doctrinal misconceptions and recovering lost benefits is one way to frame this book's purposes, there is another: to introduce church leaders, congregants, and other students of the faith to an ancient teaching that aims to change human lives. With roots going back through the Protestant Reformers to Augustine and then to the Gospel writers, to Paul, and ultimately to the Old Testament, many have seen "justification by works"—the idea that we can earn our way into God's favor— as one of the world's deepest problems, a dungeon to which God's grace alone holds the keys. Indeed, for the Protestant reformers, this problem runs so deep that it distorts the very society commissioned to help heal it: the Christian church. Accordingly, they sought to reform the church—and as they did, a clarifying idea at the center of their most insightful work was that the church itself does not save. Neither does the king, they declared, nor does the power of the sword. Neither does a particular teaching or secret wisdom. Neither, finally, does the one who has been lost, and is now found. The doctrine of election teaches that God alone saves, and that God does so through a simple, beautiful, primordial pattern that human beings, created in God's image, also embody when we love one another: we choose, elect, single out, embrace. Once we come to truly understand this, this ancient argument goes, once we believe that we are chosen and loved by God in this way, our lives will never be the same.

It is as Jesus said. Would you like to know what brings joy to heaven, to the angels of God? It is not the ones already safe and sound saying, "Amen!" No, it is the lost ones being found. "Which of you, having a hundred sheep and losing one of them, does not leave the ninety-nine in the wilderness and go after the one who is lost until he finds it? . . . Or what woman having ten silver coins, if she loses one of them, does not light a lamp, sweep the house, and search carefully until she finds it? When she has found it, she calls together her friends and neighbors, saying, 'Rejoice with me, for I have found the coin that I have lost'" (Luke 15:1–10). Election is like that because God's love is like that. God chooses, and finds, and saves, and rejoices—all in a beautifully, irreducibly personal way. Indeed, in a book about a Christian doctrine, it's worth emphasizing that the heart of Christian life doesn't consist in doctrines. Rather, at the heart of Christian life is a person—or rather, three-persons-in-unity, the triune God. Doctrines are helpful to the extent that they point toward God, God's love, and what God wants us to do and to be—the mysteries of the faith around which Christian life turns. These mysteries can never be fully explained or resolved. They can only be honored, encountered, preserved, and explored. That is what doctrine is for.

With this in mind, my argument runs as follows. Part I, "Election: An Overview," begins with a summary of the doctrine itself, starting with the basics in chapter 1, "An Ecstatic Opening." Regrettably, one of those basics is the fact that throughout Christian history, the doctrine often has been distorted and misused. Election is primarily about God, not the elect; but unless we're careful, we repeat past mistakes and project the same punitiveness and pettiness onto God that we harbor in ourselves. Examples of such projection are legion, but a particularly poignant and devastating case stands out: Christian relations with Jews. To rebuild a sound election doctrine for the twenty-first century, then, we may find no better starting point than the Hebrew Scriptures themselves. In the opening pages of Genesis, for example, we find an ecstatic, electing, creating God bringing the universe into being, and choosing, calling, and creating all of humanity in God's image—a kind of "general election" fundamental to human life. Creation's story, we might say, begins with an election as wide as the world itself. God's vision for creation is soon violated, however, first by humanity evading God, and finally by blood (Gen 3–4). In the terrifying story of Cain and Abel, we catch our first glimpse of how misunderstanding election and the electing God can lead to pride, anxiety, and division—and conversely, how understanding election well can lead to humility, assurance, and companionship.

Chapter 2, "An Apocalyptic Finish," explores three ways the New Testament frames the idea of election: how the life and teachings of Jesus give distinctive precision to God's loving search for human beings; how church practice makes election concrete in personal and social life; and finally how the mysterious event of Jesus' transfiguration epitomizes what the election doctrine proclaims. The communal dimension of predestination, properly understood, helps cultivate humility. The sacrament of baptism, and particularly infant baptism, embodies God's profound call to companionship, reminding us of how interdependent we are with families, friends, colleagues, and other neighbors. And remembering Christ's apocalyptic transfiguration provides assurance that Jesus is indeed the Elected One for whom the world waits.

Part II, "Election Up Close," includes four chapters focused on the doctrine's primary benefits: chapter 3 on how stories of the patriarchs in Genesis point toward election as a source for companionship; chapter 4 on how Israel's liberation from Egypt and the subsequent events at Mt. Sinai point toward election as a source for assurance; chapter 5 on how the Hebrew prophets point toward election as a source for humility; and chapter 6 on how Paul's exposition of election in Romans 8–12 brings these three benefits together in a single vision for the church turning outward toward our neighbors in love and respect.

Part III, "Out in the Open," explores in more detail the ways in which these ideas may take shape in the daily, weekly, lifelong practices of Christian disciples and congregations. Chapter 7, "Election on the Ground," turns to examples of the doctrine in action, as well as how the teaching has been handed down—and critiqued—in Reformed communities, and must be revised again today. Finally, chapter 8, "Election Goes to Church," focuses on ecclesial practices of Sabbath-keeping, celebration, and being commissioned into the world. Recovering the doctrine of election can invite us to sabbatical serenity even in the midst of turmoil, and in turn, Sabbath-keeping can help us more deeply experience the doctrine's riches. Likewise, in the light of the doctrine of election, Christian worship may be understood more clearly as a celebrative practice of being sent into the world, always turning outward to love and to serve. And as we have seen, a definitive case study of this kind of outward turning is Christian-Jewish relations. Following Paul in Romans 8–12, we conclude with how the doctrine of election, properly understood, gives us grounds for profoundly affirming and respecting our Jewish neighbors—and by extension, our neighbors who belong to other religions, or to no religion at all.

Books are always best engaged in conversation, and accordingly, this one concludes with discussion questions designed to facilitate doing just that. An appendix reconsiders a classic mnemonic acronym in Reformed circles for understanding the doctrine of election (TULIP), and a list of suggestions for further reading will help interested readers delve even deeper into these ancient treasures. Indeed, Christian doctrines are works of the church addressed to the church, a conversation across the centuries.

To the extent that Christian communities today reclaim that venerable teaching sometimes called "election," other times "predestination," the great conversation of our faith will be better for it: more humble, more assured, and more companionable, better able to be better neighbors to the wider world we are called to serve.

PART I

Election: An Overview

─── *Chapter 1* ───

An Ecstatic Opening

There is much we do not need to know, but one thing we must know is the basic nature and meaning of God's electing and our election.—Karl Barth[1]

THE INTERNATIONAL MUSEUM OF the Reformation in Geneva, Switzerland, includes an exhibit entitled "The Banquet of Predestination." A long table is set for an elegant dinner, with fine china and glassware at each of the ten empty places. The invisible dinner guests are significant leaders within the multiple reform movements that roiled sixteenth-century Europe. Some believed in predestination, some didn't; the doctrine's defenders had differences; and each articulates a distinct point of view. As the banquet begins, a light brightens over a first dinner plate, then a second, and so on, as we hear audio of actors playing each person at the table. The exhibit dramatizes a conversation, reasonably passionate, about a doctrine that has comforted, electrified, and disturbed believers and unbelievers for centuries.

This book is an invitation to pull up a chair and join that conversation. If you are hearing about the doctrine of election or predestination for the first time, bless you. The teaching needs revision, and you will have nothing to unlearn. You will be less likely, for example, to repeat the common mistake of skewing election's focus overmuch toward the elect. On the contrary, its prime focus is on God.

If you know enough about the doctrine to disbelieve it, bless you. The table needs your critical perspective—and believe it or not, election is the Christian doctrine that takes the pressure off all of us when it comes to doctrinal disagreements. For election is the doctrine that doctrine does

1. Barth, *Church Dogmatics*, 160.

3

not save us. Only God—working normally through church teachings and practices, but not confined by them—can do that. It's not that doctrine is unimportant; only that it doesn't save. So don't leave the election conversation; stay with us. Your critique may help push the doctrine to recover its essence, or take a new form for a new day.

But perhaps you know something about election, and happen to like what you know. Bless you—and be prepared to revise your thoughts in light of what you learn along the way. To become a Christian is to join an inquiring faith. To be a "disciple" of Jesus is basically—using the word's original meaning—to be a learner or inquirer. The church has indeed been blessed with doctrinal truth; yet an accompanying truth is that the church does not so much possess the truth as seek it. I have been impressed by the number of times in the Gospels that the disciples are portrayed as distracted or missing the point, even with Jesus in their midst. Some of faith's mysteries are elusive, even to the best of us. We shouldn't be surprised, then, to find Christian doctrines improved, developed, or clarified over time—and predestination is arguably one of the most discussable, challenging doctrines in the entire Christian treasury.

So come, take a seat at this diverse dinner table, and let's talk basics. What is this ongoing conversation all about? What are the stakes of the discussion?

The Basics

In the Christian religion, what do we mean when we say a person is "saved"? What does salvation include? How are Christians to understand it, and how is that understanding to shape our everyday lives? What is the role of God's will in salvation? What is the role of human will? How is the love, mercy, and transformative liberation of God—in a word, God's grace—distributed among human beings? Come to think of it, apart from Jesus, does anyone deserve it?

Most Christian traditions affirm that salvation includes both being accepted or embraced by God (a state of affairs sometimes called "justification") and being formed by God over time into a version of ourselves better reflecting who we truly are, God's child created in God's image (a process sometimes called "sanctification"). Accordingly, most Christian traditions affirm that it is God who decisively does the saving, not humanity. But if this is true, then in some sense God chooses—or "elects"—whom to save.

4

How should we understand this divine decision, this "election" of those who will be saved? On what basis does God decide? And what is the scope of salvation? Does God save some people and not others? Or will a good and gracious God save everyone in the end?

These are lively, controversial, and even dizzying questions—and the doctrine of election is an attempt to answer them. One stream of Christian thought, the Reformed tradition in which I stand, has emphasized strongly that salvation cannot be earned; rather, it is entirely gracious, an undeserved gift from God. To be sure, human beings participate in this salvation, but only on the basis of God's gifts in the first place. A person may "choose God," and this choosing is quite real and authentic, but she does so because God has first chosen her, giving her the power and inclination to choose God. This way of conceiving things emphasizes that God's loving choice or "election" always precedes our choosing, our acting, our good behavior, and so on. A person is chosen by God prior to her believing or doing; in this sense, from her point of view, her ultimate destiny is established ahead of time. She is "predestined." Indeed, given God's nature as eternal (that is, in some mysterious way beyond time itself), we may even say that the chosen are elected before time, before there is anything at all, "before the foundation of the world" (Eph 1:4).

Some contend that God's decision to elect a person or community is owed not solely to God but also to actions of the elect—a revision of Reformed doctrine often termed *synergism*, implying that divine and human energies somehow blend to work together in salvation, such that both parties deserve some credit in the end. A chief problem with this view, however, is that it conflicts with the posture of giving all honor and glory to God alone, as the tax collector does in Jesus' parable of two kinds of prayer (Luke 18:9–14). The religious leader in the parable pompously thanks God for making him honorable and excellent, thus congratulating himself, while the tax collector claims no honor at all. Jesus' point is that there is a one-sided asymmetry to grace, and therefore to salvation. The tax collector does mention himself in his prayer, but only as a potential recipient of God's mercy.

Picking up on this one-sided asymmetry, the early church philosopher Origen of Alexandria was among the first to emphasize the significance of the Apostle Paul's strong preference for imagery of depth and descent over what was then much more popular imagery of height and ascent in framing

Christian teaching.[2] In the Hebrew Scriptures and in Jesus, Origen insisted, the grand spiritual project of climbing toward heaven is turned on its head. History pivots not on what we have done or will do, but rather on the fact that God elects, God chooses, God "comes down" to us. Grace is, by definition, asymmetrical. It cannot be earned or deserved. It involves no quid pro quo. In later centuries, great Christian teachers—Augustine of Hippo, Thomas Aquinas, Martin Luther, John Calvin, and many others—followed suit. The Reformed preacher and so-called "first modern theologian," Friedrich Schleiermacher, framed the matter in terms of a person's "feeling of absolute dependence" on God. Each in his own way, these thinkers thought through the doctrine of election, casting salvation as a baffling, miraculous given. It comes from the other side, we might say, unearned and unbidden. It manifests as a gift, not a purchase or a trade. Everything depends, as Paul puts it, "not on human will or exertion, but on God who shows mercy" (Rom 9:16). A completely undeserved, gratuitous blessing, salvation frees the believer for God and for others.

But who receives this salvation, this free and undeserved gift of grace? Many? Few? Everyone? Over the centuries, the majority in Reformed traditions have answered this question by saying that the elect are a subset or remnant of humanity. These dinner guests quote passages of Scripture that seem to say that God saves only a few among the nations (for example, see Matt 25:31–46). Others argue that God loves all and will save all. These "universalists" at the dinner party cite different scriptural passages that seem to say that God intends to save everyone, and will not be denied (for example, see Col 1:19–23).

I am wary of a tendency in these positions—both the "remnant" view and the "universalist" view—to fall into a fundamental mistake: drawing a circle of the saved around a particular community, whether that community is a subset of humanity or humanity as a whole. When it comes to salvation's scope, humble discretion is advised. The basic choreography of the New Testament itself provides a model: those who met Jesus and were compelled by him were marked by assurance and hope. On one hand, they became more and more convinced that God was coming near to them, speaking to them, rescuing them, electing them, "saving" them. And yet, on the other hand, those very meetings were permeated with a sense of humility and mystery

---

2. See Siedentop, *Inventing the Individual,* chapter 5.

6

creatively, differently interpreting the salvation history of ancient Israel—and while sibling rivalry may be understandable, the day has come for brotherly and sisterly love. The doctrine of election should never be distorted in the service of contempt, and Christian repentance in this regard must begin with the enduring stain of Christian anti-Judaism.

With this in mind, the task of rebuilding a sound election doctrine may find no better starting point than Hebrew Scripture, from which Christians have curated a distinctive collection we call the Old Testament. The idea of election suffuses these texts, just as it does the New Testament—and accordingly, as we develop a doctrine of election unstained by anti-Judaism, the primary "textbook" we need is the Bible. In its opening pages we find an ecstatic, electing, creating God, followed by—lo and behold—the original sibling rivalry in the story of Cain and Abel, in effect the first instance of "replacement theology" in the biblical narrative. In these ancient stories, we will get our first glimpses of how misunderstanding election can lead to pride, anxiety, and division; and conversely, how understanding election well can lead to humility, assurance, and companionship.

Ecstasy and Freedom

The election doctrine's history has been marked by turbulence—more so, perhaps, than any other Christian teaching. The tensions around the doctrine, around who is "chosen" and who is not, are conspicuously apparent in Holy Scripture itself, featuring in some of the most well-known biblical stories. "Listen!" cries the older brother in the parable of the Prodigal Son. "For all these years I have been working like a slave for you, and . . . when this son of yours came back, who has devoured your property with prostitutes, you killed the fatted calf for him!" (Luke 15:29–30). The Prodigal Son is the doctrine of election in parable form. But that sibling rivalry echoes the original one in the opening pages of the Bible—and to set the scene for Cain and Abel, it's best to begin at the beginning.

In Genesis 1 and 2, we encounter an extraordinary vision of God, the cosmos, the earth, and humanity. To the philosopher's classic question, "Why is there something, and not nothing?," the first creation story provides the Bible's answer: a lyrical portrait of a God who, rather than remain self-contained or "turned inward," so to speak, instead ecstatically elects to create the cosmos, to bring galaxies and solar systems and planets into being, to give life to creatures on earth, and then finally, with care and gentleness, to make a strange sort of being, a kind of viceroy fashioned in the image and likeness of God. In the brilliant morning light of creation, the dignity and equality of every human being is lifted as high as may be imagined: all are made in the *imago Dei*, the image of God. Differences in creed, clan, and religion are not mentioned. What is mentioned is what God's *imago* on earth is to do. Humanity is God's own representative amidst creation: the air we breathe, the animals, the forests, the meadows, the seas, the mountains. Just as God is not content to be "turned inward" but rather turns outward, creating and caring for the world in love and service, so humanity is made to be a steward, a custodian, a caregiver, and in the second creation story, a gardener. The word *ecstasy* literally means "to stand outside oneself" in sheer joy, and in this sense, ecstasy is both God's signature and, in our own way, humanity's fundamental role in creation. To be entrusted with goods belonging to another, and to turn outward in joy toward caring for them, is the calling of every human life (Gen 1:28–2:4).

These creation stories illumine a dimension of election often downplayed, but essential to understanding the doctrine: "general election," according to which all of humanity is chosen, called, and created in God's image.[8] General election is the permanent backdrop to that "special election" of the people of Israel and her Messiah, and special election quickly moves to center stage in the biblical story. But that story begins with an election as wide as the universe itself. Everything that is, from the stars above to the soil below, is given—and re-given, every instant—as a gift. The world is not simply *there*. Just like Adam and Eve, we don't exist out of our own power alone. Whatever is true, beautiful, and good is God's gift; it is *created* and *given*, like a work of art joyfully presented as an expression of love. In this way, God is portrayed as outrageously generous and frequently delighted—indeed, ecstatic—about creation, repeatedly declaring it "good," and finally as "very good" (Gen 1:31).

The story leaves no doubt as to who is the sovereign, driving agent in the drama, but this only makes more striking the creation of creatures who have their own freedom and agency. Humanity shares in—or reflects, as in an image—divine freedom. Accordingly, human freedom is inalienable. Subsequent stories in Genesis consistently feature God speaking to human beings in ways that confirm the integrity of human freedom, such as posing a question or waiting for an answer (Gen 2:18–23; 3:8–13). Indeed,

---

8. To my eye, no one has grasped general election in Genesis better than William Greenway in his *For the Love of All Creatures*.

the very act of dialogue itself evokes a picture of two agents engaged in the freedom of communion. From the beginning of the biblical witness through to the end, God's majesty and human liberty go together. Even as it encourages believers to focus on divine agency as primary in the process of salvation, the doctrine of election affirms human freedom as well. In the school of the church, aided by the experiential, pictorial, and metaphorical language of Scripture and worship, election doctrine never denies the reality of human agency; rather, it aims to dissolve any inordinate, arrogant sense of human *merit* that may arise from that agency. In one justly famous summary, human beings are to work out our salvation "in fear and trembling; for it is God who is at work in you, enabling you both to will and to work for his good pleasure" (Phil 2:12–13). Are you and your agency at work? Yes. Is God at the same time at work in you? Yes. This is no zero-sum game. Is one of these agencies primary? Yes. God's agency is primary at every turn, since God is the source of all good things, including human agency itself. When you do good work, it really is your doing—but at a deeper level, your action really is God "at work in you."

In this way, the doctrine of election addresses from the outset the objection that "predestination" must involve an annulment of human freedom, as if it is a kind of coercive determinism. This would be true if divine agency were just a bigger version of human agency, since in human affairs, we take for granted that if I am the free author of a particular action (say, picking up a stone), it cannot also be that you are the free author of it. In this way, we typically conceive human agency as a mutually exclusive, zero-sum state of affairs. Even if you and I "cooperate" to pick up the stone, we can still determine how the labor was divided between us—and my contribution is my action, not yours. To the extent that we think of God's agency according to this mutually exclusive model, predestination does seem to annul human freedom: if God is the one choosing which path we take, then we are not. We're following the path, but not of our own accord. Our hands are tied; we are not free.

But divine agency is radically different from human agency with respect to at least three key dimensions: time, space, and modality. First, as the author of time itself, and therefore as somehow beyond time or, as we say, "eternal," God is not limited to temporal sequence, to "befores" and "afters," or to what we experience as past, present, and future. With respect to time, God is sovereign. Likewise, second, as the creator of space itself, God is potentially present everywhere and anywhere, both within us and without us. With respect to space, God is sovereign. And accordingly, third, as biblical stories frequently testify, the modes of divine presence and activity—particularly with respect to the Holy Spirit—include mind-boggling forms of intimacy and communion, defying the commonplace rules of mutually exclusive agency. God "indwells" human beings; "abides" within human beings as life and breath, and calls on us to "abide" in God (John 15:4). God works through us and our actions, often in ways we don't understand—all without extinguishing human freedom, identity, and integrity. Indeed, so far from extinguishing human agency, modes of intimacy with God in fact constitute human agency in the first place. That is, human freedom, identity, and integrity are themselves ongoing gifts from God, and most fully come into their own in our lives when God is "with us and through us" in the intimate freedom of communion. In other words, as we shall see, being "predestined" by God does not annul human freedom, but rather fulfills it, releasing us to walk the path God has laid out for us since before the foundation of the world—in short, to fulfill our destiny, even as God works in us and through us to do just that. Thus to conceive our lives as "predestined" is not to consign ourselves to a deterministic prison, but rather to stake a claim that, by God's grace, we are free of all manner of supposedly coercive determinisms (genetic, familial, behaviorist, socioeconomic, fatalist, sinful, and the rest) precisely because God, the sovereign in whom "we live and move and have our being," is free to overcome such constraints (Acts 17:28). Despite appearances, the past need not determine the future. In ecstatic communion with God, standing "outside ourselves" in joy and for that very reason fulfilling our true identity, we are free.

Ecstasy and Agony

From this cluster of themes—freedom, constraint, communion, identity—the story of Cain and Abel emerges; and this story, the opening episode of human life outside the garden of Eden, has everything to do with election. The first family's oldest child is Cain, a tiller of the ground like his father, continuing the troubled relationship between humans (in Hebrew, 'adam) and the earth ('adamah) that resulted from the fall (Gen 3:14–19). Cain's name (qayin), a pun on the Hebrew word for "acquire," is linked to metallurgy, music, and production; he is later credited with building the world's first city (Gen 4:17). What is Cain trying to acquire? Since this is the episode immediately following the exile from Eden, the overall gist of the family saga suggests that he wants to acquire divine favor—and sure enough, the story of Cain and Abel unfolds accordingly. Cain's younger brother, Abel, has a name with an ominous meaning in Hebrew: "emptiness" or "transitoriness." Abel is a shepherd, a job less prestigious than farming, often falling to the younger son.

"In the course of time," both brothers bring offerings to God from their respective livelihoods (Gen 4:3). Cain brings a gift from the ground, and Abel a firstling from his flock. As the older son, Cain may be assuming that his offering will be given priority. But God "has regard" for Abel's offering rather than Cain's. No explanation is given. Cain is furious. Just as the elder brother in the Prodigal Son is confounded by the father's apparent favoritism for the younger son; just as Joseph's elder brothers can hardly contain their resentment about their father's gift to his youngest son of a many-colored coat—Cain is consumed with jealously and anger. This reaction, far from a human image of God's ecstatic love and care, is rather the opposite: Cain's "en-stasy," we might say, stands not "outside himself" but rather firmly and fervently "inside himself," turned not outward in love but inward in egotism—and it's not difficult to understand why. Throughout Scripture, the theme of perceived favoritism recurs again and again, and on the surface, such favor certainly can seem unfair. But divine election is finally a love story, and love stories always involve the act of favoring, of singling out, of choosing the beloved—and such stories illustrate a profound intuition regarding God's relationship to the human community as a whole.

Is Abel chosen because his offering was somehow better? Over the centuries, many interpreters have thought so. Some focus on Cain's fruit or vegetable offering, arguing that an animal sacrifice such as Abel's was inherently superior. Others speculate that Abel brought a better portion of his offering ("the firstlings of his flock"). But if either of these theories were true, why would the author of Genesis 4 leave obscure such a pivotal detail? Yale theologian Miroslav Volf discerns a logic behind the choice, arguing that God is responding to Cain's nature as a "taker"—a child of his parents, after all—over against Abel's as a "giver." But Abel is equally a child of his parents, and again, the storyteller is conspicuously silent regarding this alleged difference in character between the brothers. In fact, each of these speculative explanations misses the heart of the narrative.[9]

---

9. On the other hand, regarding the essence of human beings as beloved children of God the Giver and Forgiver, Volf's book is a profound work. See Volf, *Free of Charge*, chapter 3.

The story's surprise is the lack of explanation itself, the fact that Abel and his offering are not presented as superior, morally, liturgically, or otherwise. But as we will see, the Cain and Abel narrative is only the first of many stories of conflict between siblings set off by God's mysterious choice to elevate one of them to apparent primacy. Cain's failure lies not in the offering he brought. As God goes on to make clear, his failure lies rather in his reaction to what he interprets as unjust favoritism.

Look at yourself, Cain, God says. *Why are you so angry?* "If you do well, will you not be accepted?" (Gen 4:7). Like a foil, God's question exposes Cain's underlying anxiety about acceptance, and the degree to which he is focused on himself. The son of Adam misinterprets his situation as a zero-sum game, as if God's embrace of Abel somehow will exclude him. Driven by this anxiety and self-absorption, and at the same time succumbing to a terrible form of pride, Cain invents his own "replacement theology," his own ideology of "supersession." Abel must go. "Sin is lurking at the door," God warns—but Cain recklessly barrels ahead. With an innocent sounding proposal to "go out into the field," he maneuvers Abel away from human habitation, out where the young shepherd will be most vulnerable to violence (Gen 4:8). Once alone with his brother, Cain kills him. Self-obsessed anxiety begets arrogant pride, and pride begets division, violence, and murder.

At its heart, the story of Cain and Abel is a cautionary tale about how destructive a malformed doctrine of election can be. Cain is created in the image of an ecstatic, loving, generous, creative God; but his acquisitive obsession with divine favor makes him act not ecstatically, but en-statically; not lovingly, but contemptuously; not generously, but jealously; and finally, not creatively, but destructively. Mistaking God's grace and acceptance for a zero-sum game can give rise to anxious covetousness, which in turn can pave the way for angry, arrogant competition and violence. In contrast, God's response to Cain outlines the antidote: a doctrine of election that begins in humility (*Why has your countenance fallen? Can you not celebrate your brother's acceptance?*), continues in assurance (*Will you not be accepted?*), and culminates in companionship (*You are your brother's keeper*) (Gen 4:6–10).

But the story also highlights at least two other key features of how the drama of election plays out on the ground. First, Cain may well have thought divine favor would mean advantages, benefits, special protections—but as Abel's fate shows, like that of Job and Jesus, God's favor in a fallen world guarantees no special protections. No shield against suffering is provided. This difficult dimension of the teaching has been clear since its beginnings. It almost doesn't matter where you look in Scripture—at young Isaac, who goes under Abraham's knife by God's command (Gen 22), or at Joseph, sold into slavery by his brothers (Gen 37), or at David, whom King Saul repeatedly attempts to kill (1 Sam 18), or at John the Baptist, arrested and put to death by Herod (Matt 14), or at the Israelites as a whole, or indeed at Jesus himself—the overarching message is consistent. The elect of God are all in the company of Abel. And second, the other side of the Cain and Abel narrative may be equally important. Cain is cursed for his unspeakable act—but in the end, God cares for him and protects him from harm. However we finally decide to classify Cain, this much is clear: the supposedly "non-favored" ones in these stories are not thereby alienated from God. They, too, receive God's love and kindness. The purpose of election has never been to benefit the chosen alone.

In short, to be one of God's elect is no road of ease and luxury; far from it. Properly understood, the biblical portrait of election is an occasion not for smug triumph, but rather for true humility and prayer. Likewise, to be one of the non-elect in these stories—to be Cain, or Joseph's elder brothers, or the elder sibling in the Prodigal Son parable—is no road to perdition; far from it. The non-elect are not abandoned by God, and as we shall see, in the Bible election typically follows the pattern of a few ecstatically chosen for the sake of the larger whole. In this way, the doctrine of election can and should be a humbling, reassuring counterpoint to Cain's anxious arrogance. Enriched by other passages on the same theme, we can almost hear God saying: *Listen to me, Cain. I am the God of your parents, and I am your God. There is a wish in your heart to be the only son, and you are angry. Listen to me. Acting on that wish will bring you nothing but damage. Wait and look. You are not the only son. But like Abel, you are my son, Cain. You are my son, and you are your brother's keeper.*

A call to humility and assurance—and in the end, to companionship. Abel's acceptance is not Cain's rejection. God's covenant with the Jews sits alongside God's covenant with the church, not in competition with it. At its best, the doctrine of election forms Christian community as a humble, poised, ecstatic celebrant of the goodness of creation in all its variety, walking hand in hand with Jews, with Muslims, and with a thousand others besides. To understand more fully how this is so, in the next chapter we turn to the New Testament and the story of Jesus' transfiguration.

--------- *Chapter 2* ---------

An Apocalyptic Finish

Despite the early church's modesty about itself, it is possible to perceive in the Synoptic writings intimations of the vast astonishment that these fisher folk and tax collectors and servants of the rich must have felt as they grasped the fact that they have been chosen for this mission. Their very identity already speaks volumes about the primary thrust of their message: sheer gift! "I thank thee, Father, Lord of heaven and earth, that thou hast hidden these things from the wise and understanding and revealed them to babes; yea, Father, for such was thy gracious will" (Matt 11:25–6).—Douglas John Hall[1]

JUST AS THE OLD Testament opens with the theme of election, casting creation as God's act of loving ecstasy, and humanity's stumble into sin as our self-absorbed "en-stasy," so the New Testament casts salvation as a grand reopening, a return to ecstasy, a recovery of our vocation to live "outside ourselves" in joyful love and service. This good news has at least three aspects. First, Jesus is himself figured as the Elected One—so to the extent that human work plays any pivotal role in election, it is Jesus' fully human work that matters. Second, the church receives two sacramental ways to cultivate conscious participation in Jesus' election: baptism and Communion. And third, all of this is conveyed to humanity not as a reasoned, doctrinal deduction, but rather as a glorious *apokalypsis* or "revelation," an event epitomized by the story of Jesus' transfiguration. In this chapter, we explore each of these aspects in turn.

---

1. Hall, *Thinking the Faith*, 59.

The Elected One

As Matthew, Mark, Luke, and John tell it, the central drama of Jesus' life can be summarized as a single question: Was he the Elect One of God, the Messiah, "the Anointed One"? The New Testament as a whole answers this question, of course, in the affirmative. A divine voice rings out at his baptism, "You are my Son, the Beloved; with you I am well pleased" (Mark 1:11). Precisely as such, however, Jesus also stands in the company of Abel. He is "favored," but he is also rejected, abandoned by his friends and followers, and ultimately killed. After three days, his resurrection vindicates not only his identity as the Elected One, but also his public ministry, including his teachings on election itself.

At the outset of that ministry in Luke's Gospel, Jesus visits a synagogue in his hometown of Nazareth on the Sabbath. The scroll of Isaiah is given to him, and he zeroes in on these lines: "The Spirit of the Lord is upon me, because he has anointed me to bring good news to the poor. He has sent me to proclaim release to the captives and recovery of sight to the blind, to let the oppressed go free, and to proclaim the year of the Lord's favor." After sitting down, the customary posture for teaching, he tells the congregation: "Today this scripture has been fulfilled in your hearing"—which is to say, *These words apply to me, here and now. I am the Anointed One, the one upon whom the Spirit of God sits, the one sent to proclaim the gospel of freedom and divine favor* (Luke 4:16–21). Throughout his ministry, he returns to this theme like a touchstone. Rebuking arrogant religious leaders, as if anticipating arrogant Christians to come, his teaching on election is a refining fire, a stringent call to humility. But when confronting filial misunderstanding and hurt, Jesus articulates the same teaching with merciful love, offering assurance and companionship—as he does in the parable of the Prodigal Son, a gentle, challenging appeal to the religious leaders of his day to join the celebration of God's abundant, unmerited grace (Luke 15:11–32).

Indeed, the Gospel writers, different as they are in temperament and details, all converge around a central message: God's salvation isn't only announced by Jesus; in some mysterious way it happens in and through the person of Jesus himself. If his teachings are the work of an apocalyptic prophet, complete with his declarations of God's kingdom breaking into the world here and now, and of the nearness of the end of the age—at the same time he himself is a kind of *apokalypsis*, a revelation of God's kingdom, not only the herald but also the presence of the new era now dawning. In short, Jesus is the Elected One. God chooses and loves and embraces him, as a parent chooses and loves and embraces a child. "You are my Son, the Beloved; in you I am well pleased." And as we shall see in the chapters to come, election has a classic, ancient pattern: the one (or the few) is elected for the sake of the many. Jesus' anointing isn't for his benefit alone, of course, or for the sake of his initial circle of followers alone. It's for the benefit of all creation. When Jesus arrives, not only supposed insiders but outsiders, too, may proclaim with confidence: "Today salvation has come to this house" (Luke 19:9).

Water and Bread

How is this so? How can Jesus' status as the Elected One benefit humanity? First, by liberating us from our en-static obsessions with earning our way into God's favor, as if we can become a member of the elect by our own work. Indeed, the whole question of being or becoming "a member of the elect" is entirely reframed by the idea that Jesus is the Elected One, the Son of Humanity, the fully human being who offers, prays, and works with genuine righteousness. For Christians, this idea opens up a new avenue for humility: now the offering, praying, and working is carried out by Jesus, and our role, in turn, is not to act on our own but rather to vicariously participate in his action, name, and presence. According to this way of thinking, if any of us claim "credit" or "merit" for such offerings, prayers, or actions, we misunderstand our actual situation. To the extent that we do participate in Jesus' life and work, we are part of what Paul calls "the body of Christ," such that "it is no longer I who live, but it is Christ who lives in me" (1 Cor 12:27; Gal 2:20). By God's grace alone, we commune with Christ in this way. Properly conceived, these ideas deepen our humility, since our good works and good standing are not ours, but Christ's. Likewise, these ideas may strengthen our sense of assurance, since they attest that our salvation does not depend on our own strength and excellence, but on Christ's. And finally, they also may enliven our sense of ongoing companionship, both with Christ himself and with the church, the gathered community, Christ's incarnate, corporate body.

A second way Jesus' status as the Elected One may benefit humanity is through the manifestation and cultivation of these ideas in the church's practical, sacramental life. To become a Christian is to be baptized into union with Christ and thereby into membership in Christ's body, the church. Accordingly, the sacrament of baptism in general, and of infant baptism in particular, is a potent teaching moment for the election doc-trine. Anyone desiring to behold a kind of experiential parable of election itself—performed as a familiar stage play, and in real time—need look no further than a Christian worship service that includes an infant baptism. Even in my admittedly reserved Presbyterian approach to worship, there is a splendid, ecstatic, engaging drama at the heart of the rite; the ceremony's "optics" are compelling and evocative. In the instructions from my denomi-national worship handbook, one direction is telling: "Care should be taken to assure that the baptism is fully visible to the congregation."[2]

And what do we see? Whether by sprinkling or by immersion (Eastern Orthodox priests routinely dunk infant candidates three times in the font!), the lesson in baptism is twofold. First, baptism is a threshold, a washing that is also a birth into new life, "in the name" of the triune God. And second, the infant is clearly a child of God and—well, an infant. Not only would she die without an affirmative and supportive community around her, her acceptance into the community obviously has nothing to do with the merit of her achievements or good work. On the contrary, the sacrament is an announcement of God's gracious embrace of the child prior to any "good work" whatsoever. The washing and the welcome is a preemptive, unearned gift. In this way, the rite is a visible sign that God is choosing her, electing her, a revelation of sheer love and grace. As the German theologian Diet-rich Bonhoeffer puts it, the sacrament is a kind of apocalyptic sermon, a revealing of God's good news: "the sacrament is the Word of God, because it is proclamation of the Gospel . . . the promise of forgiveness of sins makes the sacrament what it is, clear revelation."[3]

Other corporate dimensions of election are embodied in a second sacrament honored widely throughout the global church: the celebration of the Lord's Supper. Here the church regularly cultivates the commu-nity's participation in Christ's body, indeed its identity as Christ's body: we receive the Body in the rite in order to become the Body in our lives, again and again. This has to do with being commissioned into the world, of course, going in peace to love and to serve. But it also has to do with our self-understanding as incorporated into the body of the Elected One. We "take and eat" the Communion bread and cup, in part so we can say, with Paul, "Christ lives in me." We gather around Christ's table, in part so we can experience our collective identity as "the body of Christ," the body of the

---

2. *Book of Common Worship*, 7.

3. Bonhoeffer, *Christ the Center*, 52–53.

Anointed One, God's child, "the Beloved" in whom God is "well pleased." In a sense, all of Christian worship is an exercise in this new identity formation, participating in Christ's Body, as Christ's Body. Likewise, we pray not in our own name, but "in Jesus' name," the name of the Elected One on whom God's favor rests. Properly understood, such practices should humble and assure us, and at the same time release us from en-static anxieties about climbing our way up into God's favor. There's no need to climb. God has already, graciously come down.

There are no guarantees here, of course; sin's ingenuity knows no bounds. Christians can still convince ourselves, even as we pay lip service to Jesus and humility and God's grace, that we are nevertheless earning our way into divine favor: that our "faith in Jesus" deserves salvation; that our dutiful attendance in worship deserves salvation; indeed that our baptism itself, or our earnest celebration of Communion, deserves salvation. And if someone reminds us that orthodox Christian teaching points in the opposite direction, that our faith and worship are themselves gracious gifts of the Holy Spirit; that baptism and Communion portray Jesus, not us, as the true source of agency and merit—then we may well insist, as a kind of last resort, that our admirably orthodox Christian *teaching* about faith and worship deserves salvation. Surely God will look favorably upon our impeccable doctrine, especially the one about how we cannot earn God's favor!

And so it is precisely here that the doctrine of election makes its last stand. Election is the doctrine that doctrine will not save us. Only God can do that. Only God saves—not our efforts, not our good works, not our worship, and not our orthodoxy. God saves. And the force of calling this teaching "predestination" is this: God chooses, elects, destines human beings for salvation before any of our efforts or works or worship even get underway, before our orthodoxies are established, before our doctrines are written. Like infants being baptized, we receive God's love before we know it, before it even occurs to us to "earn" it. And this effectively reframes all of these things—works, worship, doctrine—not as actions we carry out in order to win our way into God's arms, but rather as actions we carry out in gratitude and joy that we already are there, that God already has acted with breathtaking, merciful grace. God's love comes first, preempting all of our action, "predestining" us to divine acceptance from the very first—just as a loving parent's care precedes everything the child does (indeed, even precedes her birth!). In the light of this teaching, our whole lives may be lived in gratitude and joy. Our self-centered en-stasy may open up into ecstasy, into living "outside ourselves" in joyful love and ministry.

Revealed Glory

In my case, I felt the value and larger importance of the election doctrine long before I could explain it, even to myself. I first sensed it in gatherings for worship in Christian congregations. It was there that I heard a message along these lines: "Come. You are the one. Now." Inside the sanctuary, election names the most intimate and precious experience imaginable in life with the Spirit. The psalm comes alive: "Happy are those whom you choose and bring near, to live in your courts" (Ps 65:4).

Such experiences may be informed by doctrine, but they are not exercises in doctrinal deduction or reasoning. They can only be felt, sensed, intuited. Remember: election is a love story, and love cannot be logically deduced; it can only be revealed and experienced. Likewise, the idea that Jesus is the Elected One cannot simply be inferred from other teachings, or proven from some set of supposedly universal premises. Rather, it belongs to the sphere of *apokalypsis* or "revelation." If the doctrine of election begins in the Old Testament with ecstasy, its development in the New Testament comes down to apocalyptic disclosure: God revealing that Jesus, this particular human being in this particular time and place, is the Elected One, the Beloved in whom God is "well pleased."

At the center of this apocalyptic theme in the Gospels is the story of Jesus' transfiguration, the cathedral dome, we might say, in the architecture of the New Testament (Matt 17:1–8; Mark 9:2–13; Luke 9:28–36). Disciples "will do well," as the author of 2 Peter puts it, recalling this extraordinary incident, "to be attentive to this as to a lamp shining in a dark place, until the day dawns and the morning star rises in your hearts" (2 Pet 1:19). As Mark tells the story, Jesus hikes up a high mountain, taking Peter, James, and John with him. On the mountaintop, Jesus is suddenly "transfigured before them," his clothes becoming "dazzling white, as no one on earth could bleach them." Elijah and Moses appear, talking with Jesus. The disciples are understandably terrified; Peter stammers a suggestion, offering to build "three dwellings" for the three luminaries—but just then, a cloud rolls in, and a loud voice proclaims of Jesus, "This is my Son, the Beloved; listen to him!" Elijah and Moses vanish, and Jesus alone stands before the disciples (Mark 9:2–13).

For our purposes here, the transfiguration is the doctrine of election condensed into a single story. Its primary message is that Jesus is the Elected One. Radiance, obscurity, and confusion pervade the scene, of course, signaling that we are dealing with a great mystery; but at the same time, the chaos functions to make the passage's foreground even more vividly clear. Without denigrating Moses and Elijah, and in fact exalting them, the story's spotlight falls on Jesus, the beloved Child of God. Predictably, the disciples' initial instinct is to do something, anything, that would somehow match the moment: hosting them in dwellings, or building them shrines—but all of that, it turns out, is beside the point. The point is that Jesus is the Elected One.

The scene has an apocalyptic atmosphere, and not only because Elijah, the figure whose return was then thought to herald the end times, is present. The otherworldly clothes, the mysterious cloud, the thunderous voice, the disciples' fear—these details all point to a theophany, a revelatory appearance of God, and a clarification of divine purposes. In Matthew, Mark, and Luke, the event serves as a kind of anticipation of the resurrection appearance stories that come later, a glimpse of future glory. And at the same time, the event also serves as a profound act of assurance, a pep talk to raise the disciples' morale—since the descent to the cross is about to begin. But most of all, the story's overall effect is a sudden, clear, dazzling announcement, an *apokalypsis* declaring that Jesus is the Elected One. This status cannot be doctrinally inferred, or even discerned through careful examination of his life or his ministry. It must be divinely revealed. Accordingly, Christians cannot gaze too often up into that cathedral dome that is the transfiguration. It is a heavenly vision: amidst indescribable light, Jesus humbles us, assures us, and then invites us to accompany him down into the valley below—to Golgotha, yes, but also beyond Golgotha, to the heavenly, earthly, astonishing glory of the empty tomb.

But note this well, as we gaze up into this Christian dome: Jesus, the Elected One, is talking collegially with two of Israel's most revered leaders, Moses and Elijah. Even as it spotlights Jesus, the scene is a resounding affirmation of Paul's case in Romans that to the Israelites "belong the adoption, the glory, the covenants, the giving of the law, the worship, and the promises; to them belong the patriarchs, and from them, according to the flesh, comes the Messiah" (Rom 9:4–5). And indeed, by the same token, the scene is also a vivid, humbling portrait for each and every Christian, and for Christianity writ large. For at the center of the tableau is a man we would describe, were

PART II

Election Up Close

─────── *Chapter 3* ───────

Companionship in Genesis

> It was not because you were more numerous than any
> other people that the LORD set his heart on you and
> chose you—for you were the fewest of peoples. It was
> because the LORD loved you and kept the oath that he
> swore to your ancestors . . .—Deuteronomy 7:7–8

AT THE HEART OF the doctrine of election lies a puzzle. If human merit
is not the basis for why God elects to save a person, or a people, or a nation—then what is the basis for that decision? Indeed, what else could it be,
if salvation is to be fair and just?

The puzzle is instructive because it springs from at least two false
premises. First, it presumes that salvation is "fair and just." But the doctrine
of election centers on the idea of grace—and grace, by definition, is neither
"fair" nor "unfair." Grace is a free, undeserved gift of forgiving love. It is not a
reward or a payment, and what's more, precisely as forgiving love, it presup-
poses that there is something amiss—either a violation or a state of estrange-
ment, or both—that needs to be forgiven, reconciled, or otherwise repaired.
Indeed, viewed through a lens of justice, grace can seem unfair. But grace is
not a kind of justice; grace is a kind of love. Second, the puzzle presumes that
salvation is retrospective, that God looks back and assesses a person's (or a
people's) life, or at least a major part of it, and dispenses salvation to those
whose performance deserves it. On the contrary, however, the doctrine of
election moves in the opposite direction: God's election is prospective, not
retrospective. It happens at the outset, looking forward. Like a parent's love,
election always comes at the beginning of the story.

To see how this is so, we need look no farther than the stories of
the patriarchs and matriarchs in Genesis. In this chapter, we turn first

to Abraham—arguably the paradigmatic account of election for both Judaism and Christianity—and finally to Joseph. Like bookends, these two sagas open and close the patriarchs' narratives in Genesis, introducing and confirming a doctrine of election with an array of potential benefits for humankind, not the least of which is to expand and strengthen the companionship in our lives.

Commissioned to Companionship

The story of Abram (whom God later renames, "Abraham," or "father of a multitude") stands at the headwaters of Israelite tradition, the first story after the so-called "Primeval History" of Genesis 1–11. As a classic account of God choosing a person, and through that person, a people, Abraham's saga includes many lessons about the doctrine of election—and the first such lesson jumps off the page at the outset. For the story doesn't begin as we might expect it to begin, with a parade of flattering episodes demonstrating how Abram is "a good and righteous man." In fact, we learn virtually nothing about Abram at all. And yet, God elects him. God loves and chooses and calls him. The implication is clear: Abram's election isn't "earned" or "deserved." It's not a reward for good behavior; if it were, the storyteller would say so. Rather, Abraham's election—and by extension, election generally—is a gift.

A second lesson is that Abram's election isn't merely a decision in God's mind, so to speak, with effects only on God's side of the relationship. Rather, Abram's election happens in time and space, and in particular, as it unfolds, it takes the form of a particular kind of call: a commissioning. God doesn't simply love Abram and elect him and inform him of that fact. God sends Abram on a mission. To be loved in this way, to be elected, is to be sent on an adventure: "Now the LORD said to Abram, 'Go from your country and your kindred and your father's house to the land that I will show you'" (Gen 12:1). According to this paradigmatic story, the form election takes in human life is a summons, explicit or implicit, to embark on an unfolding mission, a journey with plenty of surprising twists and turns.

A third lesson is that this mission is to be carried out for the sake of blessing. Variations of the term "blessing" appear no less than five times in these three verses (Gen 12:1–3). But these blessings are not only, or even primarily, for Abram. The point of the mission is to bless others as well: speaking to Abram, God promises to "make of you a great nation," and ultimately that "in you all the families of the earth shall be blessed" (Gen 12:2–3). As we have seen, the creation stories in Genesis outline what is sometimes called "general election"; here in Genesis 12, we see God's "special election" of Abram and his descendants. But note well, the "special" is ultimately for the sake of the "general." Just as in the story of Noah, in Abram's story the spotlight narrows to a single individual in a single family in a small town in Mesopotamia—and it does so precisely for the sake of "all the families of the earth." Election is never only or even primarily about benefiting "the elect"; rather, it's about blessing the whole of creation, and above all, it's about the blessed breadth and depth of God's graceful mercy, God's merciful grace.

For Abram, then, God's call amounts to a commissioning to companionship: companionship with his family and descendants and neighbors, to be sure (indeed, "all the families of the earth")—but also companionship with God. This is a fourth lesson to be drawn from Abram's story. God does not send him on this adventure alone, but rather promises to accompany him along the way. The partnership is epitomized and memorialized in an agreement, a covenant, sealed in a ceremony. God promises blessings and commissions Abram; Abram trusts and obeys the One who calls him. Thus we can expand the definition of election represented by this saga: election is a commissioning to an adventure undertaken in covenantal companionship with God. Finally, a fifth lesson is that this adventure, and this companionship, will be extraordinarily challenging. It will involve learning, growth, and maturation—which is to say, it will involve difficulty. God does indeed say, "Do not be afraid, Abram, I am your shield," but as the story goes on to make clear, such protection does not exempt the elect from pain, suffering, and trial (Gen 15:1). On the contrary, the patriarchs' stories in Genesis suggest the opposite. After all, no adventure is worthy of the name without its share of trouble. The call to companionship, then, is also a call to struggle, and it can even be a call to the crucible of a harrowing ordeal.

So it was with Abraham. His saga concludes with one of the most famous—and infamous—passages in Scripture, the story of the *Akedah* or "Binding of Isaac" (Gen 22:1–19). God tests Abraham by commanding him, in an echo of the original commissioning, to "go to the land of Moriah" and offer his son, Isaac, as a sacrifice (Gen 22:2). As with the opening of the story of Job, the storyteller tips the reader off at the outset that this drama is actually about a test, not a killing. Nonetheless, since Abraham does not yet know this, the story proceeds on a razor's edge. Abraham rises early in the morning, saddles his donkey, and takes Isaac and two young men with him. They cut wood, and then set out toward the place God shows him. On the third day, as they approach, Abraham turns to the young men and says, "Stay here with the donkey; the boy and I will go over there; we will worship; and then we will come back to you" (Gen 22:5).

This line is beautifully rendered, with various shades of meaning. On one level, Abraham hides his sacrificial intention from Isaac and from the young men. On another level, ironically, the words intended to conceal and pacify turn out to be true. And on yet another level, the words suggest that perhaps Abraham is still hoping that somehow the worst will be avoided. In this story, as in our lives, the relation between human plans and God's plans are subtle and complex. Human intentions and divine intentions interweave, diverging and converging in ways virtually impossible to untangle. Likewise, when they come near the spot, Isaac says, "The fire and the wood are here, but where is the lamb for the burnt offering?" Abraham responds, with precise ambiguity, "God himself will provide a lamb for a burnt offering, my son" (Gen 22:7–8).

Soon Abraham arrives with Isaac at "the place that God had shown him." Dialogue ceases. The action slows down to show Abraham's astonishing trust: building the altar, binding Isaac, and reaching out to take the knife in his hand. The moment has come—and as it does, heaven intervenes. As the angel arrives in the nick of time to stop the appalling sacrifice, there is a sense in which we readers already know what is going to happen. The angel is going to speak—not physically block the knife, as some painters have chosen to render this scene. The angel is going to call Abraham by name. Then the angel is going to stop talking, wait for an answer, and receive an answer. How does the attentive reader know all this in advance? Because an intervention in exactly this form has already taken place in the story—twice. As the story opens, God says to Abraham, "Abraham!" And he replies, "Here I am." As they make their way up the mountain, Isaac says to his father, "Father!" And Abraham says, "Here I am, my son." And now, at the story's climax, an angel calls from heaven saying "Abraham, Abraham!" And he says, "Here I am." The angel continues, "Do not lay your hand on the boy or do anything to him; for now I know that you fear God, since you have not withheld your son, your only son, from me." Abraham looks up, sees a ram in a thicket—and offers the ram on the altar "as a burnt offering instead of his son" (Gen 22:12–13).

the people of Israel. As we will see, both Moses and Israel exhibit repeated, deep-seated insecurities about their elected, commissioned life with God—and accordingly, the portrait of election in Exodus emphasizes how God consistently, powerfully reassures them. From this angle, we may define election's covenantal companionship with God as a pathway of continual assurance. Along the way, we'll encounter two special problems: first, the mystery of how divine and human agency are related; and second, the unconditional-yet-conditional character of election. To help make sense of these puzzles, we'll explore the notions of "efficacious grace," "justification," and "sanctification"—ideas which turn out to be keys for how the doctrine of election can deepen and strengthen healthy forms of human confidence.

The One Who Draws Out

The first sign that the exodus story will pivot around the tension between insecurity and assurance is the way the story begins. A new king comes to power in Egypt, one who "did not know Joseph," and institutes a new regime of oppression against the Israelites (Exod 1:8–11). And at the same time, the story suggests that the Israelites have lost confidence in God. According to Abraham's story in Genesis, the Israelites are enslaved in Egypt for 400 years—and in Exodus, what sets their liberation in motion is that they "cry out," and God hears them (Exod 2:23–25). The story's implication, then, is that they had not cried out before; that they had grown resigned to their circumstances, and lost confidence that they—or the God of their ancestors—could change those circumstances for the better. Even their "cry" in the Exodus story isn't necessarily addressed to God. It's a groan, a cry of sheer anguish.[2]

But God hears the cry, and God acts. God "remembers" or "takes notice" of the covenant with Abraham, Isaac, and Jacob (Exod 2:24–25). In the fullness of time, the story suggests, God's sovereign purpose never fails. As we have seen, God has already elected Israel, and now a new chapter will open up in that commissioned companionship. A more elaborated covenant will be sealed at Mount Sinai—but God does not summon all the Israelites

---

2. Walter Brueggemann puts it this way: "the cry is neither God-induced nor God directed. The beginning point of the exodus is rooted not in any explicitly theological claim, but in this elemental fact that human bodies can absorb [only] so much . . . Perhaps this God is especially sensitive to cries of oppression." Brueggemann, "Exodus," 706.

at once. As in the foundational story of Abraham, God begins with a single figure, whom God will commission for the sake of the whole.

Moses' name means, "the one who draws out," a wordplay initially linked to the fact that the Pharaoh's daughter draws him out of the water, where his mother had shrewdly placed him to avoid the Pharaoh's murderous decree (Exod 2:1–10). But of course a deeper meaning of this name is that Moses will be chosen and commissioned by God to be "the one who draws out" the Israelites from Egyptian enslavement, including "drawing them out" of the waters of the Red Sea in their climactic escape from Pharaoh's pursuing armies. The deepest meaning of the name, however, is how it points to God's activity, which underlies and animates every step of the story. In Exodus and beyond, God is indeed "the One who draws us out" from our various forms of captivity, choosing and commissioning one or a few for the sake of the many. And in some mysterious way, as in the story of Moses, this choosing and commissioning happens "before" we know it, preceding all we think and do. When Pharaoh's daughter took hold of that infant boy, lifting him out of that basket floating in the Nile and naming him "Moses," the one who draws out—how could he have known? His calling, his destiny eventually will become clear to him, but only over time, through an extended and arduous discovery.

Like his people, Moses is insecure, anxious, and afraid. After killing an Egyptian taskmaster for beating one of his fellow Hebrews, he flees into hiding. He takes up the quiet life of a married shepherd in the countryside, having apparently left Egypt behind for good. But he's restless. One day he leads his flock "beyond the wilderness"—a striking, enigmatic phrase—and finds himself at "Horeb, the mountain of God," a peak traditionally identified with Mount Sinai itself (Exod 3:1). It's there that he sees a burning bush, turns aside to take a closer look, and comes face-to-face—or face-to-fire—with the Electing God of his ancestors.

Throughout the exodus story, Moses is the Elected One, "Exhibit A" for the book's argument about the meaning and purpose of election. God does lead and guide Moses, to be sure; but even more, God shapes and forms and tests him. When asked, God takes the unprecedented step of an introduction by name: "God said to Moses, 'I AM WHO I AM' [or 'I AM WHAT I AM,' or 'I WILL BE WHAT I WILL BE']. God said further, 'Thus you shall say to the Israelites, 'I AM has sent me to you'" (Exod 3:14). God then takes this new intimacy with Moses a step further, revealing a second name ("YHWH," often rendered in English Bibles as "the LORD"), which practice of assurance and reassurance, a weekly rhythm of participating in God's shalom, remembering God's creative power, and appreciating that the world is, indeed, "very good" (Gen 1:31). To the extent that the other six days of the week have ground down our sense of confidence and security, the sabbath may help build it back up. The sabbath, we might say, is a day of remembering our election, the foundational good news that God loves and commissions us, and walks with us as we go. Sabbath-keeping is a distinct footprint of God's people in the world of time.[4]

The other weekly—and even daily—practice of intimacy and assurance Israel receives at Sinai is worship itself. When the people arrive at the mountain, a kind of dialectical tension opens up. On one hand, God seems awesome and terrifying: "thunder and lightning" swirl around the people, and a "thick cloud" descends on the mountain, accompanied by "a blast of a trumpet so loud that all the people that were in the camp trembled" (Exod 19:16). On the other hand, this very God is the Electing One who has chosen Israel precisely and explicitly for the intimate companionship worship entails. Indeed, the opportunity to worship God has been an explicit aim and purpose woven through the entire story: "Let my people go," God says, through Moses, to Pharaoh, "so they may worship me in the wilderness" (Exod 7:16; 8:1).

To this daily and weekly rhythm of worship and sabbath-keeping, God and Moses add another: the annual cycle of festivals, and in particular, the festival of Passover each spring. "Seven days you shall eat unleavened bread," Moses tells the Israelites even as they are leaving Egypt, commemorating how they had no time to add leaven to the cakes of dough they brought with them. On the seventh day, Moses continues, "there shall be a festival to the LORD"—for the power that released them from Egypt, after all, was God leading "by strength of hand" (Exod 13:6,3). Remembering this strength every year in a grand festival is a practice of assurance *par excellence*, an annual reminder that, whatever forms of captivity we may experience, God is a God of strength and deliverance. Throughout the exodus drama, God shapes and forms every side: when a particular plague of locusts, boils, or darkness fails to soften Pharaoh's heart, it is because God has hardened it; when Israel takes a particular step toward liberation, it is because God has empowered them to take it. We may build our hope, our assurance, our confidence on no more compelling ground than this: that the God who

---

4. Abraham Joshua Heschel has masterfully captured the lyrical and lifting power of sabbath for the elect community, and for the world, in his masterpiece *The Sabbath*.

once liberated our ancestors from enslavement shall do the same again for us, and indeed is doing so even now.

With all this in mind, at Mount Sinai, God has Moses tell Israel that they are now elect in a full and complete sense of the word: "You have seen . . . how I bore you on eagles' wings and brought you to myself. Now therefore, if you obey my voice and keep my covenant, you shall be my treasured possession out of all the peoples. Indeed, the whole earth is mine, but you shall be for me a priestly kingdom and a holy nation" (Exod 19:4–6). In this declaration, three elements essential to the covenantal companionship between God and God's people come into view. The first is God's gracious act of choosing and deliverance: "I bore you on eagles' wings and brought you to myself." As it turns out, the Israelites' crucial destination on this journey is not the wilderness, nor the Mountain of God, nor even the promised land on the horizon. No, the destination is nothing less than the divine presence: God has taken Israel up "and brought you to myself," which is to say, to an ongoing, elaborate intimacy with God. Such has been the true aim of the exodus all along.

The second element is that God's promise is linked to a demand: "if you obey my voice and keep my covenant, you shall be my treasured possession out of all the peoples." God's election of Israel in the first place is sovereign and unconditional, but in some mysterious way, the ongoing covenantal relationship is conditional, as all covenants are. This unconditional-yet-conditional character of election presents a special problem—and opportunity—we'll explore in the next section below. In any case, however, framing covenantal companionship as a conditional imperative makes Israel's status endlessly contingent, and thus never possessed outright as an entitlement; it is always a divine gift. Finally, the third element is a clarification, underscoring again that the purpose of election is not to benefit the elect alone. If Israel is "holy," set apart, they are expressly singled out in order to be "a priestly kingdom"—and a priest, of course, is a vicar whose work is done to benefit not himself alone, but vicariously to benefit the people as a whole: "all the families of the earth," as God puts it to Abram, or indeed "all the peoples," as God now puts it to Moses, for "the whole earth is mine" (Exod 19:4–6).

justification and sanctification can itself be a source for reassurance amidst the winding twists and turns of the life of faith.

In biblical covenants, we frequently find ourselves encountering the tension between, on the one hand, a profound divine mercy that forgives "seventy times seven" and, on the other hand, a majestic, overwhelming divine sovereignty that will not be mocked. At one and the same time, God unconditionally embraces us, and makes challenging demands of us. And for good reason: the covenantal companionship commissioned at Sinai begins a new chapter in Israel's story, but it is not a chapter of unbroken intimacy and trust. Election calls us to continual companionship and continual assurance—but it also calls us to continual humility. We turn now to that grand, consummately humbling biblical tradition, which Moses initiates: the Hebrew prophets.

―――――― *Chapter 5* ――――――

Humility in the Prophets

Indifference to evil is more insidious than evil itself; it is more universal, more contagious, more dangerous . . . The knowledge of evil is something that the first man acquired; it was not something that the prophets had to discover. Their great contribution was the discovery of the evil of indifference. One may be decent and sinister, pious and sinful. —Abraham Joshua Heschel[1]

IN THE PATRIARCH'S NARRATIVES in Genesis, election is cast as an unearned gift, a commission to covenantal companionship, God's act of choosing one family lineage for the sake of "all the families of the earth." In the exodus story of liberation, that companionship is cast as continually reassuring, including a set of confidence-building practices—legal and liturgical— meant to make possible an entire way of life with God. Insofar as a doctrine of election underscores these themes, it may substantially contribute to enhancing Christian companionship and assurance. But it can only do so if it also delivers on what is arguably its primary purpose: to deepen and strengthen Christian humility. Without humility, election doctrine is a clanging cymbal. Arrogant Christian companionship is no companionship at all—but rather, paternalistic contempt. Hubristic Christian assurance is no assurance at all—but rather, self-absorbed entitlement.

Diarmaid MacCulloch ends his magisterial history of the sixteenth-century European reformations with a lament.[2] Westerners today are likely to be puzzled—if not repulsed—by the Reformation, he writes.

1. Heschel, *The Prophets*, 64.
2. MacCulloch, *The Reformation*, 706–8.

Christians were prepared to burn and torture one another on doctrinal grounds, because they disagreed, for example, on whether or precisely how bread and wine were transformed into God's presence. Surveying post-Reformation carnage within Christendom, Reinhold Niebuhr once remarked: "In its treatment of those who differed from its interpretation of the Gospel, [the Reformation] was singularly barren of the humility which betrays 'the broken spirit and the contrite heart' . . . [I]t never submitted the doctrine of justification by faith to the experience of justification by faith."[3] Niebuhr's point is devastating: in one of the tragic ironies of Christian history, the *experience* of being gracefully chosen and embraced by God not because of one's actions, but despite them, too often has been eclipsed by the weaponization of the *doctrine* of justification by faith. After 500 years, the Reformation is in need of a reset.

But Niebuhr's critique itself, humbling as it is, contains a remedy. The doctrinal disease of weaponization has been around for centuries, even millennia—but so has its doctrinal antidote. As we have seen, election is the doctrine that doctrines will not save us, including, at the top of the list, the election doctrine itself. A person's relation to God is decided by God. Only God saves, and so the life of faith rests on God's graceful election, not on our faithfulness. In this way, grasped rightly, the doctrine of election shines a bright light on the dark side of all religious doctrine: its capacity to create a sense of "possessing" the truth, and its consequent liability to being used in campaigns of contempt, indifference, and violence. Nowhere is this bright light more searing than in the Hebrew prophets, and any sound doctrine of election must pass through this prophetic tradition of self-critique, radical humility, and, when necessary, indignant rebuke. To borrow Niebuhr's formulation, the doctrine of election must be submitted to the experience of election.

The Prophetic Tradition

Who is a prophet? We may begin with Moses at the burning bush, and God's revealing response when the shepherd protests that he lacks eloquence. "Who gives speech to mortals?" God asks. "Now go, and I will be with your mouth and teach you what you are to speak" (Exod 4:11–12). The prophet, first and foremost, is a person who speaks on behalf of God, who delivers a divine message. "Thus says the LORD" is the signature of prophetic speech.

3. Niebuhr, *Nature and Destiny*, 226.

What does a prophet say? In short, words of consolation and words of condemnation. But what is striking about the words of condemnation in the Hebrew prophetic tradition is that they are typically addressed not to Israel's enemies, but to Israel itself. This is the stream of reproving discourse most characteristic of the biblical prophets: they are the voices who turn to Israel with words of warning, admonishment, rebuke, and denunciation. The prophetic tradition is the voice of Israel's self-critique—that is, God's critique delivered through Israel's own messengers—about what has gone wrong in the covenantal companionship with God, what is going wrong in it, or what is about to go wrong with it. At its heart, prophetic speech is a call to return to the covenantal path, a stern warning to a partner who has gone astray. In this sense, it is a tradition of course correction, of seizing our attention so we can get back on track.

But the prophetic critique also runs deeper. One of the most frequent and iconic targets of the prophet's condemnation is idolatry, essentially the act of putting something else—another god, an institution, oneself—in the place of God. From the point of view of covenantal companionship, the way of life for which God has elected Israel and has made possible through the miraculous rescue from enslavement, no other charge could be more serious. Idolatry is the ultimate act of ingratitude, insolence, and entitlement. It represents a drastic misunderstanding of one's actual situation as a beneficiary of God's love and grace. And most importantly, it consequently leads to severe distortions of the covenantal community itself, the kind of society God lays out in the Torah, since arrogant entitlement with respect to God inevitably involves arrogant entitlement with respect to one's neighbors. Idolatry amounts to an abandonment of the covenantal companionship to which divine election calls and commissions human beings. It desecrates and corrupts human community. And God, the prophets declare, will have none of it.

What is most startling about this condemnation, however, is how the prophets so often apply it not to the wayward outskirts of Israelite life and society, but to its very core, its most prestigious and well-educated precincts. The rulers of Israel, the prophets insist, have lost their way, forgetting "the widow and the orphan"—which is to say, neglecting the most vulnerable members of society. And most striking of all, the religious leaders of Israel have lost their way, their worship of God not just corrupt but mistaken. God wants none of it, neither their songs nor their ceremonies nor their sacrifices; instead, God wants Israel to "do justice, and love kindness, and kingdom"—may or may not be won. Such pictures are typically summative, pulling important threads together into a final bow—and accordingly, this is the last lesson Jesus formally offers in Matthew's Gospel, the teaching note he chooses to end on. It comes at the close of a three-chapter run on the theme of judgment, and immediately before Matthew's three concluding chapters on Christ's passion, crucifixion, and resurrection. A critical turn in the preceding section is the beginning of Matthew 24, where Jesus leaves the temple and the crowds who had been listening to him there. After cautioning his followers that even massive and impressive buildings like the temple are only built with stone, and that one day "all will be thrown down," Jesus retreats to the nearby Mount of Olives. His disciples "came to him privately" with questions about the end times: *When would the temple be destroyed? What would be the sign that Jesus was who he said he was? When was the end of the age coming?* (Matt 24:1–3).

Jesus' answer concludes with this story. When the "Son of Humanity comes in his glory" and sits on his throne as "a king," everyone will be gathered before him, and, "as a shepherd," he will separate the sheep from the goats. The sheep, he says, have performed works of love and mercy: feeding the hungry, giving drink to the thirsty, welcoming the stranger, clothing the naked, caring for the sick, and visiting the prisoner—all iconic expressions of the prophetic insistence on serving the most vulnerable, and on the idea that God desires "steadfast love and not sacrifice, the knowledge of God rather than burnt offerings" (Hos 6:6). In contrast, the goats have done no such thing. The king reveals that when the sheep served those in need, in fact they were directly serving him, feeding him, welcoming him, and so on; and when the goats didn't, they weren't. Accordingly, the sheep are welcomed into "eternal life"; the goats, to "eternal fire" (Matt 25:31–46).

This is a story about election, and at first glance—and indeed, as it is often understood today—it appears to construe election as a matter of righteous action and reward. And yet, on closer inspection, this is precisely what the story does not say. When the king summons the sheep, he says, "Come, you that are blessed by my Father, inherit the kingdom prepared for you from the foundation of the world; for I was hungry and you gave me food . . ." (Matt 25:34–35). At least three factors point to the idea that the sheep's election is not based on their righteous action, and rather that their righteous action is based on their election. First, "the kingdom" the sheep will inherit was "prepared for you from the foundation of the world." Here again, we encounter the core meaning of the "pre-" in "predestination": it means "before" any of our action takes place, and so it rules out the very idea of election being a reward for good behavior. Thus Jesus excludes at the outset the notion that God waits to see what we will do, and then dispenses awards and punishments accordingly. Second, Jesus addresses the sheep as "you that are blessed by my Father"; God's blessing is already in place, prior to this gathering before the king. And third, a point so obvious that it's easy to miss: the sheep are already sheep in this story, created by God as such, prior to their lives and actions. This isn't a story about separating good sheep from bad sheep; this isn't a separation based on behavior. Rather, God's blessing is given at the very beginning, effectively making the creature who she is (a sheep!), a fact the creature owes solely to God's creative generosity in the first place.

In other words, the story paints a picture of a world in which "sheep"—by their given nature, which is to say, by God's graceful gift—perform works of love and mercy. Such actions are themselves blessings of God, flowing from God's election, not the basis on which that election is decided. The king's remark, "for I was hungry and you gave me food" does not mean, "I have elected you *because* when I was hungry you gave me food," but rather "I have elected you, and *indeed*, when I was hungry you gave me food."[7] The services described—feeding, welcoming, and so on—demonstrate the creature's election in the first place, the divine favor established "from the foundation of the world." Thus Jesus rejects the idea that election is a reward. Every truly righteous action, this story declares, is itself an indication that election has already happened. Works of love and mercy are the fruit, not the root, of God's saving grace.

And for this very reason, they are no cause for pride. Thus Jesus affirms the prophetic emphasis on serving the vulnerable, while at the same time doubling down on the prophetic exhortation to humility. Have you performed works of love or mercy, as God, through the law and the prophets, has commanded? Good for you—but don't you dare conceive those actions as reasons to puff yourself up with arrogance. On the contrary, turn to God in humility and thanksgiving, since those works of love and mercy—both the opportunity to do them and the ability to do them—are graceful, undeserved gifts from God. The more good works we do, the more humble we should become.

7. The Greek word in play here, *gar* ("for"), is variously translated across the New Testament, including both as "because" and as "indeed"—which is to say, as expressing the cause of a preceding event or idea, or as expressing the continuation or elaboration of a preceding event or idea. The word "for" has a similar semantic range in English.

Beginning at the End

Romans 12 begins a section of the letter devoted to Christian life, with advice that paints a portrait of ideal Christian disciples as Paul conceives them: "living sacrifices" with transformed, renewed minds; honorable, loving, ardent, and patient; eschewing haughtiness and retaliation, and living in harmony with all (Rom 12:9–21). This second section of the letter is clearly distinct from the first—but it is not separate from it. On the contrary, the second section begins with a clear reference to the theological work immediately preceding it: "I appeal to you therefore, brothers and sisters . . ." (Rom 12:1). On that "therefore" hangs a crucial insight. When Paul appeals to his readers—including us—that we "therefore . . . be transformed by the renewing of your minds," he refers to the intellectual, existential, spiritual renewal he's just described in chapters 8–11 (Rom 12:1–2). That is, with this "therefore," Paul points to his exposition of the doctrine of election.

In other words, for Paul, the doctrine of election is no esoteric, merely cerebral exercise. It is a teaching intended to animate and shape Christian life, to be learned, grasped, and acted upon. It is meant to transform and renew our minds, and so to help guide and inspire who we are and what we do, making us more honorable and loving, humble and harmonious. Early in the Christian movement, the Letter of James was written as a warning against spiritual distraction, and as a reminder that "faith by itself, if it has no works, is dead" (Jas 5:19; 2:17). Accordingly, for Paul, election is something to be lived out; God's graceful embrace ("justification") involves, as a kind of immediate effect and embodiment, embarking on a new path toward a new way of life ("sanctification"). St. Simeon, the renowned "New Theologian" of Eastern Christendom, put it this way: "Do not try to describe ineffable matters by words alone, for this is an impossibility . . . let us contemplate such matters by activity, labor, and fatigue."[1]

How might the doctrine of election, at its best, help renew our minds and lives in this way? As we have seen, in the patriarch's narratives, in the exodus story, in the prophets, and in the ministry of Jesus, election emerges as a call to companionship, assurance, and humility—and accordingly, as Paul makes his case in Romans, he weaves together these strands into an integrated whole. The problem to which election is a remedy is first introduced in chapter 7: the inner conflict between, on the one hand, a person's knowledge of the law received at Sinai (that is, knowledge of "what is

---

1. Quoted in Pelikan, *The Christian Tradition*, Vol. 2, 258.

good") and, on the other hand, that same person's inability to follow that law. The reason for this inner conflict, Paul contends, is that "the good does not dwell within me," and this state of affairs—which Paul identifies with the malign power of sin—means that even if I energetically try to keep the commandments, I inevitably find myself doing so in a distorted, counterproductive way. I may follow the law to the letter, and at the same time stray radically from its spirit. Precisely because "the good does not dwell within me," I find myself in an untenable, self-contradictory situation: "I can will what is right, but I cannot do it. For I do not do the good I want, but the evil I do not want is what I do" (Rom 7:14–25).

The obvious remedy for this predicament is for "the good" to "dwell within me"—and that is precisely what Paul declares in Romans 8 as good news for his listeners: that through the electing grace of God, "the Spirit of God dwells in you," living and acting with and through us in intimate, ongoing companionship (Rom 8:9). Like the authors of the patriarchs' narratives, Paul presents election as having no cause beyond God's sovereign love; the Spirit's indwelling isn't a reward, but rather a gift. And like the prophets, Paul zeroes in on Israel's most exalted activity, worship: "we do not know how to pray as we ought," he declares, but the Spirit both "intercedes" for us and actually prays with us and through us, so that when we cry, "'Abba! Father!' it is that very Spirit bearing witness with our spirit that we are children of God" (Rom 8:15–16). Indeed, given that Paul frames the problem in Romans 7 as an inability to follow the law and act as we ought, we might expect him to move immediately to the idea that the Spirit's indwelling enables us to model good, law-abiding behavior. Strikingly, however, he does not yet make this move. As we have seen, Paul eventually arrives at the theme of virtuous action in Romans 12, but first, even as he describes Israel's most exalted activity—worship—as an intimate act of companionship between "our spirit" and God's "Spirit," Paul takes time to emphasize two crucial themes, one at a time: assurance and humility.

It is as if Paul is saying that the inner conflict described in Romans 7 is first and foremost a problem giving rise to anxiety, and even to despair—and so his initial message to his readers is one of hope and encouragement. Fear not! Be assured! God's Spirit now dwells with you, witnessing that you are children of God. The Spirit will assist you, and when necessary, intercede for you—and since we are so intimately bound up with God, we are inseparable from God's steadfast loving kindness. Indeed, we can rest assured that "neither death, nor life, nor angels, nor rulers . . . nor anything else in all creation, will be able to separate us from the love of God in Christ Jesus our Lord" (Rom 8:38). God gave us the framework for companionship—the law—at Sinai, and though we may understandably fear that our inability to follow that law will lead to God abandoning us, in fact, God will do no such thing. For God, with infinite mercy, has elected us nevertheless, dwelling within us as God's Spirit, and witnessing that nothing, not even sin, will separate us from God's graceful, forgiving love.

Couched within this initial emphasis on assurance is Paul's most explicit evocation of the doctrine of election or "predestination." Echoing Joseph's reassuring words to his brothers, Paul insists that "all things work together for good for those who love God, who are called according to his purpose" (Rom 8:28; cf. Gen 50:20). This "working together for good" isn't divine improvisation reacting to events as they happen, Paul insists, but rather a divine symphony unfolding in time, an opus written, so to speak, beforehand: "For those whom [God] foreknew he also predestined to be conformed to the image of his Son, in order that he might be the firstborn within a large family. And those whom he predestined he also called; and those whom he called he also justified; and those whom he justified he also glorified" (Rom 8:28–30). Read in context, Paul intends this "predestination" to be a profoundly reassuring word, as if to say: *God chose you from the first, laid out your destiny from the first, and accompanies you along that destiny, all the way to the last. Take heart!*

Overall, Romans 8 is a tour de force of election doctrine: relational, assuring, and humbling. Paul casts election as a form of companionship with God—the Spirit's indwelling presence—that itself makes other forms of companionship with God possible. The fact that God has chosen us is deeply assuring, of course, as is the fact that God's choice is not based on our righteousness or lack thereof, but rather on God's steadfast love. Moreover, by describing God's decision as an act of "predestination," a symphony that's already written, Paul encourages us to lay aside any anxiety that some other power—death, life, angels, rulers—will divide us from God's grace. And at the same time, the teaching is profoundly humbling: election's genius is how it simultaneously strengthens the assurance of faith and weakens prideful arrogance. Our companionship with God is revealed as a merciful gift from God, not a result of our excellence or obedience, and so all hubris and boasting are ruled out. If the symphony of our lives includes any beauty, we have God, the composer, to thank and praise.

All our actions—the actions Paul will turn to in Romans 12—should be shaped and governed by this stance and perspective: enlivened by intimate companionship with God; grounded in equanimity born of assurance; and formed by the humbling conviction that, though we have not earned salvation as a prize, we nevertheless have received it as a gift. This is the tenor and temper of Christian life as it follows from the doctrine of election—but before Paul gets to the specific actions of Romans 12, he first lays out what he understands to be the iconic *pattern* of Christian action, the underlying choreography within which specific Christian conduct properly takes its place: *turning outward toward our neighbors in love and respect.* This pattern is good and right in any case, of course, but it is good and right first of all with respect to those neighbors who are nearest at hand, and against whom we may be tempted to turn in rivalry, envy, or resentment. For Cain, we might say, it is good and right first of all with respect to Abel. For Joseph, it is good and right first of all with respect to his brothers. And for Paul—as indeed for Christians generally—it is good and right first of all with respect to Jews.

Christian life and neighborliness with Jews is a kind of case study, then, for Christian life and neighborliness writ large, an iconic pattern to be repeated in other particular instances, again and again. But for Jesus-followers such as Paul, turning toward his fellow Jews raised a painful question, indeed one of the most painful questions of all in the days of the early church: If the followers of Jesus are elect children of God, does that mean the Jews who decide against following Jesus are not? In Romans 9–11, as a final step before Romans 12, Paul confronts this question head on.

Turning Outward

Having just declared—robustly and definitively—that nothing "will be able to separate us from the love of God in Christ Jesus our Lord," Paul now turns to the most immediate, conspicuous case that would appear to be at risk of just such separation: fellow Jews who decline to follow Jesus (Rom 8:38). Accordingly, Paul begins with "great sorrow and unceasing anguish in my heart" on behalf of his comrades, even wishing "that I myself were accursed and cut off from Christ for the sake of my own people" (Rom 9:2–3). As an apostle declaring that Jesus is the long-awaited Messiah, Paul may well be tempted to turn his back on fellow Jews who reject his proclamation—indeed all the more so because Paul believes that his

66

message is meant for Gentiles as much as Jews. But Paul does not turn inward toward the ranks of the new movement, both Jewish and Gentile. Rather, he turns outward precisely toward those who have declined to join in—and in the process, both unveils and exemplifies the graceful pattern at the heart of election.

First, Paul affirms that God has indeed elected Israel: "to them belong the adoption, the glory, the covenants, the giving of the law, the worship, and the promises; to them belong the patriarchs, and from them, according to the flesh, comes the Messiah, who is over all, God blessed forever. Amen" (Rom 9:4–5). And while it is true that many Jews have decided not to follow Jesus, Paul continues, this does not mean that "the word of God had failed" (Rom 9:6). On the contrary, at least two possibilities may account for Jesus' mixed reception. First, while God has elected Israel, precisely who counts as "Israel" is, Paul contends, a dynamic, open question. Just as God subverted expectations about who was "favored" or "elect" in the days of the patriarchs—for example, exalting younger sons over older ones, as with Jacob and Esau, or Joseph and his brothers—so God is subverting expectations about who is included in the elect community today. The central and driving argument of Paul's ministry, of course, is that God's salvation, while emerging in the first place from Jewish origins, turns outward from there, widening to include Gentiles as well. Accordingly, for Paul, God's election of Israel includes a diverse group of Jews and Gentiles together: "the children of the promise are counted as descendants" (Rom 9:6–13). So while it may appear at first glance that "God's word had failed" because significant numbers of Jews decline to follow Jesus, what's actually happening, Paul insists, is that God is revealing that Israel's "descendants" shall eventually include even greater numbers, Gentiles alongside Jews.

The second possibility is that both acceptance and rejection of Jesus may be part of God's dramatic design. Just as God actively influences both sides in the exodus story, at once encouraging the Israelites to demand freedom and "hardening Pharaoh's heart," so God is active, Paul argues, on both sides of Jesus' story: "So then [God] has mercy on whomever he chooses, and he hardens the heart of whomever he chooses," the latter "to show his wrath and make known his power," and the former "to make known the riches of his glory" (Rom 9:18, 22–23; Exod 9:12). Paul even goes on to speculate that those who decline to follow Jesus thereby open the gates to others: "through their stumbling salvation has come to the Gentiles" (Rom 9:11). This line of argument echoes Jesus' parable about a dinner party, in which the original invitees decline the host's invitation, leading the host to invite supposed out-siders, and finally to pull in people from "the roads and lanes"—and at the same time to rebuke, and apparently exclude, the supposed insiders who initially declined (Luke 14:15–24).

Taken together, these two possibilities seem to indicate that Paul's answer to the question, "If the followers of Jesus are elect children of God, does that mean the Jews who decide against following Jesus are not?" is a straightforward "Yes." God may be widening the "descendants" of Is-rael to include both Jews and Gentiles, but Jews who reject Jesus, it would seem, will be left out in the cold. Likewise, while rejection of Jesus may be part of God's overall dramatic design, even opening salvation's gates to the Gentiles—it is nonetheless rejection of Jesus, and as such is an occa-sion, Paul suggests, "to show God's wrath." Even Jesus' parable about the dinner party ends with the ominous line, "For I tell you, none of those who were [originally] invited shall taste my dinner" (Luke 14:24). By all accounts, then, Paul seems to be arguing that Jews who decline to follow Jesus thereby forfeit their ancestral election, effectively stepping outside the circle of salvation even as Gentiles are invited in. In this new world, Paul declares, neither ethnic identity nor impeccable obedience to the law are required for justification; rather, the sheer trust of "faith" is the mark of the saved: "if you confess with your lips that Jesus is Lord and believe in your heart that God raised him from the dead, you will be saved" (Rom 10:9). And sure enough, such confession and belief are precisely the things that the Jews who have rejected Jesus have declined to embrace. As we have seen, Paul is anything but clinical or detached about this news: he writes of "great sorrow and unceasing anguish in my heart" (Rom 9:2). Sentiment aside, however, for Paul, the cause of Jews outside the Jesus movement ap-pears to be lost. Whether they realize it or not, the fateful circle has been drawn—and they stand definitively outside it.

So begins one of the most extraordinary passages in the New Testa-ment, Paul's surprising turn not toward the inside of this fateful circle, the newly diverse Jesus movement, but rather toward those outside it, the very Jews for whom his heart aches. For this fateful circle, important as it is, is nevertheless penultimate. God's dramatic design has yet one more act, even more astonishing than what has preceded it. In Romans 11, hav-ing set the rhetorical stage in Romans 9 and 10 with an argument clearly placing the vast majority of Jews apparently beyond salvation's reach, Paul performs a Christlike turn outward toward his brothers and sisters. And

were unwitting "enemies for his sake" all along, and that God's hidden design was, in the end, for their sake, too, saving them from famine. Likewise, Paul recasts any Jewish rejection of Jesus as an integral part of God's overall symphony of grace. And to any Jesus-followers tempted to look down on Jews who decline to join the movement, Paul has a ready reply: "Just as you were once disobedient to God and received mercy," so they "have now been disobedient in order that, by the mercy shown to you, they too may now receive mercy. For God has imprisoned all in disobedience so that he may be merciful to all" (Rom 11:30–32). At this, Paul can only break out in ecstatic praise: "O the depth of the riches!" (Rom 11:33).

From this remarkable vantage point, and in this atmosphere pervaded by astonishment, Paul turns at last to his portrait of Christian life beginning in Romans 12. "I appeal to you therefore, brothers and sisters, by the mercies of God," to be "transformed by the renewing of your minds," to "not to think of yourself more highly than you ought," to love genuinely, to live in harmony with one another, and so on (Rom 12:1–16). The preceding discussion of how "all Israel will be saved" is not an aside or a digression, but rather a culminating case study, an iconic illustration of divine election in the light of which Christian life—humble, assured, and companionable—is properly lived out. In other words, for Paul, God's election of "all Israel" only intensifies the sense in which Christians should conduct themselves without arrogance, anxiety, or contempt for their neighbors. If the elect includes not only Jesus-followers but also people they would otherwise have deemed "enemies," then election is emphatically based on God's grace, not human works, excellence, or righteousness—with the result, for the elect, that both boasting and anxiety are decidedly out of place. Moreover, Paul's turning outward toward precisely these supposed "enemies" epitomizes the signature choreography of Christian conduct: turning outward toward our neighbors in love and respect. This is not Paul's invention, of course; the turn is profoundly Christlike, and Paul is working out its implications in this letter. God's graceful mercy sets the tone and the pattern, and Paul, at once proclaiming and exemplifying this pattern, calls upon the fledgling church to do the same. Thus the doctrine of election, as Paul lays it out in Romans 8–12, is not only something to think; it's something to do, an idea with implications for living out lives of consummate humility, assurance, and companionship.

Mercy and Blessing

Stepping back to view Paul's argument as a whole, at least four things stand out. First, Paul preserves and affirms what today are familiar marks and standards of Christian community, even as he situates them as penultimate, which is to say, as permanently subject to being superseded by divine mercy. For example, Paul declares that salvation, which occurs "by grace" and not by "works," takes the visible form of faith and confession: "if you confess with your lips that Jesus is Lord and believe in your heart that God raised him from the dead, you will be saved" (Rom 11:6; 10:9). But at the same time, those Jews who reject Jesus are precisely those who do not "believe in their hearts" or "confess with their lips that Jesus is Lord"— and yet, they, too, Paul declares, are among the elect. Does this mean that all Jews will eventually convert to Christianity? It is certainly possible to imagine that, in the end, such faith and confession will become universal in Israel and beyond, and that those "enemies" who die in the meantime will learn to believe and confess in the age to come—but that is not Paul's argument in Romans. Rather, he marvels at the wonder of including all of Israel in salvation ("how much more will their full inclusion mean!"); affirms that the "enemies" in Israel are beloved not because of some future change of heart, but rather "for the sake of their ancestors"; underscores not their future obedience, but rather God's mercy ("so they have now been disobedient in order that . . . they too may now receive mercy"); and finally simply breaks into ecstatic praise: "O the depth of the riches and wisdom and knowledge of God! How unsearchable are his judgments and how inscrutable his ways!" (Rom 11:33).

These moves accumulatively point to the idea that, as important and legitimate as faith and confession are in the formation of Christian community, as signs of election, they are sufficient but not necessary. Even those who neither believe nor confess may be numbered among the elect, if God so chooses. As Paul puts it in Romans, quoting God in the exodus story: "I will have mercy on whom I have mercy" (Rom 9:15; Exod 33:19). Since God is sovereign, from the human point of view the limits on election cannot be pinned down—the election of "all Israel" being what for Paul's community was a stunning case in point. Indeed, for Paul, every single case of election is a case of sovereign divine mercy in the face of "disobedience": "For God has imprisoned all in disobedience so that he may be merciful to all" (Rom 11:32). In this way, Paul emphatically underscores how the ultimate scope of salvation is—this side of the eschaton—a permanently open question.

God saves, and the reach of God's mercy cannot be fathomed, never mind confined within sectarian limits.

If divine sovereignty was on Paul's mind as he composed this argument, surely its corollary—human humility—was as well. For Paul, "faith" was the linchpin of his case for how Gentiles could become "children of the promise" made to Abraham: they may not have the ethnic pedigree, physical mark (circumcision), ceremonial propriety, or legal standing of observant Jews, but so long as they had faith, they, too, were heirs of Abraham, the paragon of faithfulness. But Paul was only too aware, of course, that "faith" could become as potent and prideful a weapon as any ethnic, physical, ceremonial, or moral bona fides. "I (or we) have faith, and you don't" can work quite nicely as a self-congratulatory, divisive rallying cry. "Works righteousness" might be set aside as a hubristic misunderstanding of salvation, but what we might call "faith righteousness" is close behind, ready to rush in and fill the vacuum. As we have seen, the Hebrew prophets and Jesus build protective guardrails against this temptation—Jesus' story of the Last Judgment being perhaps the best known in Christian circles today, with its surprising upshot that, in the end, the ultimate criterion will not be "faith" or "religion" after all. Likewise, here in Romans 9–11, Paul builds a guardrail of his own against the temptation to weaponize "faith." Yes, we may rightly affirm "faith in Jesus Christ" as the mark and standard of full participation in the Christian church, which is to say, the mark and standard of election—but the moment we take another step and declare this the *only* way God elects human beings, we put ourselves in a precarious position, apparently up on a pedestal, looking down on everyone else. Against this possibility, Paul emphatically counters that "all Israel will be saved," simultaneously underscoring the sovereignty of the God of mercy, rejecting the idea that the scope of that mercy can be defined in advance, and reminding us that, even as we recognize Christian faith as a divine gift, we dare not foreclose the possibility that God may have other gifts for other people.

Second, Paul's picture of election is a motion picture, a drama unfolding over time. Its origins are in Israel, and Paul draws from wellsprings in the patriarchs' narratives, the exodus story, and the prophets to make his case. But for Paul, these origins are the beginning of a much larger, expanding story—an expansion glimpsed at the very outset, in the story of the call of Abram: "in you all the families of the earth shall be blessed" (Gen 12:3). God's blessing of one family leads to the blessing of an entire people, Israel; and likewise, God's blessing of Israel shall lead to the blessing of all. For Paul, of course, the mission to the Gentiles is a crucial chapter in this larger, unfolding story—and along the way, in his own time as much as in Abraham's or Moses' time, the expanding movement meets resistance and rejection. God is inscrutably active in those countervailing dynamics as well, Paul contends, "hardening hearts" to heighten and promulgate the drama of redemption. In the end, however, God's saving mercy shall extend even to hardened hearts. Just as in the book of Isaiah, the prophet declares that Egypt, too, will ultimately experience its own exodus and deliverance, Paul declares that "all Israel will be saved" (Isa 19:20; Rom 11:26). Just as in the story of Joseph, what may appear to be setbacks or abandonment may well be, in the end, part of God's hidden design "in order to preserve a numerous people, as he is doing today" (Gen 50:20; Rom 8:28). Indeed, if the sacred memory of Israel is any guide, the last act of election's drama will be at least as astonishing as the acts preceding it.

Third, Paul communicates to his colleagues in Rome—and by extension, to us—as much with his rhetorical choreography as with his words themselves. Following the pattern at the heart of election, he conspicuously turns outward, both toward the Gentiles and toward Israel as a whole, even and especially toward those within Israel who stand outside the Jesus movement. This division within Israel, he proclaims, so painful to Paul personally, will be mercifully overcome: all Israel, even apparent "enemies," will be saved. In Paul's hands, the doctrine of election is an idea, but it is also a gesture, a continual turning outward. God gracefully opens up an avenue of justification, a road marked not by impeccable righteousness but by confession and faith in Jesus Christ—and then, in a kind of double portion of mercy, God nevertheless saves all of Israel, including those who decide against confession and faith in Jesus Christ. Contemplating this second wave of grace, this mercy overflowing the supposed limits of mercy, Paul can only exclaim in rhapsody, "O the depth of the riches and wisdom and knowledge of God!" (Rom 11:33). Far from mere ornament, this exclamation of praise is telling: it signals a high point, a limit beyond which exposition cannot go, and a recognition that the symphony of redemption is both dazzling and unexpected. Paul's explicit account of election begins in Romans 8, with his evocation of those God has "predestined," but it climbs to a crescendo with this ecstatic doxology, and with the iconic case study that inspires it. God's election of Israel is an epitome of God's election writ large. As Paul traces its pattern, he, too, effectively performs the Christlike turn outward toward his neighbors, indeed toward his supposed "enemies"—a gesture that in crucial respects sums up the proper shape of Christian life.

And finally, fourth, with all of this in mind, there is no place in Paul's argument for supersession, the idea that Christianity somehow supersedes and displaces Judaism as God's chosen people. If anything, for Paul, the dynamic is the other way around: the Gentiles in the Jesus movement are grafted into the tree of Israel—and in any case, Paul proclaims, "all Israel will be saved . . . for the gifts and calling of God are irrevocable" (Rom 11:26–29). Christianity cannot supplant God's covenantal election of Israel, or otherwise place ourselves above our Jewish brothers and sisters. To do so would be to boast, turning inward in religious self-satisfaction, not outward in neighborly love and respect. Indeed, as we have seen, the doctrine of election is a frontal attack on sectarian pride. Such pride can surface anywhere, of course, but a key place to watch for it is wherever one spiritual tradition encounters and interacts with another. For our part, when it comes to relations with Judaism, we Christians have too often behaved as a dysfunctional family—as if, like Cain, our wish has been to be God's only child, or, failing that, to be God's *favored* child. At its worst, this impulse has led to violence, as well as to contemptuous and condescending "replacement" theologies claiming Christian superiority. But in Romans 8–12, Paul sets out in the opposite direction. Not supersession but rather non-supersession is the great mystery he proclaims in Romans 11, and for a telling reason: "So that you may not claim to be wiser than you are, brothers and sisters" (Rom 11:25). In the hands of the apostle, just as in the hands of the prophets and patriarchs before him, the doctrine of election calls us to companionship even with supposed "enemies," to assured confidence in divine fidelity, and above all, to humility before God and neighbor.

What would human life formed by such a doctrine look like in our own time, out in the open for all to see? How does the teaching need to be reformed today? And how may the church best rehabilitate the doctrine for the twenty-first century? In Part III, we now turn to these three concluding questions, making the case that the doctrine of election is an indispensable idea central not only to the gospel, but also to the form of human life that follows from it.

PART III

Out in the Open

Chapter 7

Election on the Ground

There's a wideness in God's mercy, like the wideness of the sea;

There's a kindness in God's justice, which is more than liberty.

There's no place where earthly sorrows are more felt than in God's heaven;

There's no place where earthly failings have such kindly judgment given.

—Frederick William Faber[1]

ONCE WE BEGIN TO look for it, we may find election's signature pattern—the Spirit's ecstatic choreography of turning outward to our neighbors in love and respect—all around us, in both expected and unexpected places. At its best, the doctrine trains us to dance: humbled by God's graceful rescue and assured by God's steadfast faithfulness, we turn outward toward others with modesty and poise. Refusing to imagine limits for God's mercy, we see everyone we meet as a potential member of God's elect—a status that need not necessarily correlate, as we have seen, with conversion to Christianity. Accordingly, we turn outward toward others with companionable good will, seeking genuine relationships of kindness, courtesy, and honor. As we have seen, Paul paints a portrait of this kind of humble, assured, companionable life in Romans 12, using the ancient rhetorical form of a list of imperatives. But beyond such lists, what does human life shaped by a sound doctrine of election look like on the ground, out in the open for all to see?

---

1. From Faber's classic hymn, "There's a Wideness in God's Mercy," *The New Century Hymnal*, 23.

The Pope in Bosnia

One sunny Saturday in June of 2015, Pope Francis made a whirlwind trip to Sarajevo, the capital of Bosnia-Herzegovina. Riven by ethnic tensions and religious violence between Christians and Muslims, the country has a national anthem without words—because warring factions cannot agree on them. Speaking to a crowd of 65,000, the Pope called for greater religious reconciliation and an end to sectarian conflicts, which he called "a kind of third world war being fought piecemeal." Francis met with Bosnia's three presidents, one from each of the country's three minorities: Serbian Christian Orthodox, Croatian Catholic, and Muslim. "In a world unfortunately rent by conflicts," the Pope declared, "this land can become a message, attesting that it is possible to live together side by side."[2]

Here is one portrait of what a life shaped by sound election doctrine looks like in practice. The Pope's visit was no panacea, of course; it inspired palpable encouragement, but also understandable skepticism. In both of these respects, however, Francis modeled an admirable, Spirited turning outward in love and respect. One local historian and diplomat simply shook his head: "Of course, his visit will change nothing. He leaves, and our political leaders will continue to speak about nationalism and religion." Similarly, a high school student remarked, "I hope that there will be reconciliation in this country; but honestly, I do not think so. It is very hard to believe in such a thing." And yet, this difficulty—the challenge of believing in reconciliation under such circumstances—is precisely why the Pope made his visit in the first place. Turning outward toward our neighbors in love and respect is most useful in places where reconciliation is hard to believe; indeed, Paul's turn toward fellow Jews who rejected Jesus was anything but easy. The humility, assurance, and relationality inspired by election doctrine will draw us toward such difficult waters, not away from them. The Pope was in the right place at the right time, doing the right thing.

And on the other hand, even in the midst of these challenges, the optics surrounding the Pope's visit were dramatic and hopeful. As time for the outdoor mass approached, Sarajevo's streets were nearly cleared of regular traffic, as a stream of hundreds of buses poured in from across the region. Tens of thousands of worshippers moved across the city to reach the crowded stadium. What had once been known as "Sniper Alley"—a riverside road that

---

2. All quotes regarding the papal visit are taken from Lyman, "Pope Urges a Divided Bosnia to Heal," 8.

had separated Serbian and Muslim forces during the conflict—was suddenly a winding line of buses cooling in the shade of bird-filled trees. It was as if an occupying force of a different kind was arriving.

These ordinary people, too, modeled the turning outward that can be inspired by election doctrine. In bright green T-shirts, a group of students from neighboring Croatia joined the march. Their leader was a twenty-five-year-old seminarian, who put it this way: "People are frightened; they are worried about conflict. The Pope is correct that we need dialogue for there to be peace. But it does not mean that we change our doctrine, just that we talk and we try to understand each other." Between these lines we can glimpse a kind of grounded, humble, assured strength. Like Francis, the young seminarian was not fearful of having to change his identity or forfeit his convictions, nor was he insistent that his counterparts change or forfeit theirs. And for this very reason, he was open to engagement, to "talking and trying to understand each other." He was open to dialogue. He was open to companionship—not counterfeit companionship, which secretly or openly attempts to homogenize and collapse differences into sameness, but rather genuine companionship, which respects differences and seeks understanding, "side by side."

Between the Pope and the seminarian were hundreds of other religious leaders moving within the same broad, graceful choreography. The "Council of Interreligious Dialogue," formed to bring together the country's disparate clerics, had been making substantive progress. "Yes, the Council is working well," said Archbishop Luigi Pezzuto, the Vatican's ambassador to Bosnia. "Now what is needed is to translate this capacity for dialogue to all people. We need people to understand that religion is not a reason for friction. It is an instrument to resolve friction." The truth is that religion takes many forms, both divisive and reconciling. But the archbishop's point—along with the Pope's and the seminarian's—is that at its core, religion may indeed be a powerful, reconciling force in human affairs. The Christian doctrine of election, rightly grasped, can help move Christian individuals and communities in these reconciling directions, turning outward toward our neighbors in love and respect, following Francis, following Jesus.

In one of his most practical, revealing parables, Jesus invites us to picture a banquet. Never sit down, he says, at the place of honor. Why? Because you never know if someone more distinguished than you has been invited by your host, but has yet to arrive. Consider what could happen. If such a person has been invited, and then the host comes and asks you to give up your seat, in disgrace you will have to move toward a lower place. But if instead you go and sit down at the lowest place when you enter the banquet, and then the host comes and sees you and says, "Friend, move up higher," you will be honored in the presence of all at your table. The signature gesture of a person formed by a sound doctrine of election, one might say, is to make room, humbly and wisely, for others as well (Luke 14:7–11).

And by the same token, the signature gesture of a person formed by an unsound doctrine of election is the opposite: to elbow my way to the place of honor, to deny room to others, to take their place and shut them out. In its most elemental, extreme form, this distorted choreography takes shape as a desire—Cain's desire—to be God's only child, a perverse, insecure aspiration leading to "religious war" in one way or another. If open warfare and violence are ruled out, the aspiration simply shifts: *If I cannot be the only child, then let me be the favored one. Let me sit in the place of honor.* The claim to supersession, with its "replacement theology," isn't far behind. The opposite of turning outward toward our neighbors in love and respect is to turn inward toward ourselves in clannish, contemptuous pride.

Thus two roads diverge. Down one is humility, assurance, and companionship, and down the other is hubris, insecurity, and isolation. The work before the Christian church today, with God's graceful help, is not only to travel with firm resolve along the first road; it's also to clearly, candidly repent from the second. On Good Friday, for example, the day of the Christian year marking Christ's crucifixion, it is traditional to reflect on one's own sins and failings. Many churches have created liturgies to express and guide Good Friday meditations. My own Presbyterian Church (USA) proposes the liturgy that follows. The lines in bold are spoken by the congregation.

> **Holy God,**
> **Holy and mighty,**
> **Holy and immortal One,**
> **have mercy upon us.**
> I have grafted you into the tree of my chosen Israel,
> and you turned on them with persecution and mass murder.
> I made you joint heirs with them of my covenants
> but you made them scapegoats for your own guilt,
> and you have prepared a cross for your Savior.
> **Lord, have mercy.**[3]

3. *Book of Common Worship*, 290.

Election Doctrine in History

The elect are God's chosen people. As we have seen, however, the revealing question is, "Chosen for what?" For salvation? Yes—and also for participation in God's mission to redeem the world. For salvation? Yes—and also to model, with God's graceful help, a turning outward toward our neighbors in love and respect. In short, God does not save the elect *as opposed to* their brothers and sisters, as if God's mercy is parsimonious and narrow; rather, God saves the elect *for the sake of* their brothers and sisters, as if God's mercy is generous and as wide as "the wideness of the sea." Too often in Christian history, this essential pattern of the election doctrine, this echo of God's proclamation to Abram that "in you all the families of the earth shall be blessed," has been eclipsed, forgotten, or overlooked (Gen 12:3).

When Protestants today refer to "the received doctrine of election," the reference typically is to predestination as the Westminster Confession and Catechisms present it. In this context, a "confession" is an official statement of faith, and the Westminster Confession, though written in England in 1647, has played a formative role in much of the American Reformed community, from its adoption in 1729 as the confessional position of the Presbyterian Synod in the colonies right down to the present day. One of the finest of the major Christian confessions, Westminster sharpens and systematizes the teachings of the Swiss Reformation, with divine covenant and election as two central themes.

In order to see Westminster clearly, however, we must first bear in mind the distinctive role confessional statements have played in Reformed thought. In Joseph's Small helpful phrase, the Reformed have been the "most diffuse" of the four main traditions to emerge from the sixteenth-century reformations in Europe (the other three being Lutheran, Anabaptist, and Anglican), and this diffusion has been accompanied by a proliferation of official confessional statements—over sixty in the sixteenth century alone.[4] From the outset, variety has been the rule. Accordingly, while all of these confessions are considered authoritative as statements of the faith of Reformed Christians in particular times and places, the Reformed tradition as a whole has never recognized a single confession, or even a collection of confessions, as having special authority. Reformed Christians are simply too confessional to do this. Instead, they continually ask in new eras and

---

4. Small, *To Be Reformed*, 1. See also chapters 1, 4–6, 11.

circumstances: "What does the living God require of us here? What is Jesus asking of us now? How should we confess this to the world around us?"

Indeed, even the most extraordinary and beloved examples of Christian confessions have a particular place in Reformed Christianity: a subordinate one. They are subject to the authority of Holy Scripture, which in turn derives its authority from Jesus Christ, the Word of God, "the Supreme Judge, by which all controversies of religion are to be determined," discernible by way of "the Holy Spirit speaking in the Scriptures."[5] So reads Westminster itself. In other words, as prestigious as the Westminster Confession is, it is subject to the church's continual discernment, guided by the Holy Spirit, as to how well it does or does not comport with Scripture, and ultimately with the ongoing teaching office of Jesus Christ. Far from a settled matter, then, the question of how we should understand the doctrine of election is alive and well today, in our own era and circumstances—and it has been clear for some time now that the problems with the Westminster Confession are significant.

The essence of the difficulty can be summarized by way of one vivid historical example. The nineteenth-century novelist Harriet Beecher Stowe was raised in the celebrated New England clan of the renowned Presbyterian pastor Lyman Beecher, and so grew up steeped in the Westminster Confession and its predestinarian orthodoxy. After a terrible family tragedy, she became obsessed with questions of election and damnation. Her son, Henry, had died in a swimming accident while at Dartmouth College, and as far as she knew, he had not experienced a conversion—certainly not of the requisite variety. Grief-stricken, she did what every believer is entitled to do with church confessions. She used the "iron" of her heart, soul, and experience to sharpen the "iron" of her tradition's public statement of faith (Prov 27:17). Of Westminster's theology and design, Stowe wrote: "Woman's nature has not been consulted." Had it been, she insisted, the ancient view of woman as mere temptress would have yielded to a different type of insight: women are mothers of the human race. Unlike male system-builders, they are "always returning from the abstract to the individual and to feeling, where the philosopher only thinks." Had mothers been at the theological table, Stowe declared, their wisdom and grief would have put aside long ago the tortured intricacies of election and reprobation, and turned instead to the love of Christ.[6]

5. "Westminster Confession," 6.010.
6. Quoted in Thuesen, *Predestination*, 133–34.

to catch your breath from work, so you can get back to work, refreshed, in short order. It's a far deeper, more luxuriant, more celebrative form of repose: to rest "as if all my work were done." In this sense, the Sabbath day is an attack on the temptation to works-righteousness that so widely pervades the other six days of the week, the idea that we become righteous, accepted, elect, not by God's gift but by our own efforts. On the Sabbath, the work-and-reward ethos is set aside, and in its place, ideally, we lean into a gift-and-gratitude ethos, the true nature of our actual situation as children of a gracious God who cares for us all week long. To "remember the Sabbath day, and keep it holy" is to remember this truth, the deepest truth of our lives: that God has already chosen us, already loves and cares for us, already has prepared a path for us, a destiny we now walk, and will continue to walk, with God together. The saving work is done. Our efforts do not bring grace into our lives. God saves. We don't. So rest, beloved child, and live today as if all your work is done. Even more, live as if God's saving work is done—for in a profound sense, it is. God has already accomplished it, since "before the foundation of the world" (Eph 1:4).

Thus the Sabbath day is, we might say, a practice of predestination.[2] It is a day of remembering and experiencing the loving, saving grace already at the center of our lives, and doing so with all our mind, heart, soul, and strength. The Sabbath proclaims that salvation is a *fait accompli*—and at the same time provides a tangible way to experience the grace by which God has accomplished it. It is a day of resting in God's arms. There is no need to earn or strive or climb our way into divine grace, for the Sabbath day is saturated with grace, filled with signs of grace—indeed, the day itself is a gift from God, a day of grace. It is a foretaste of the messianic banquet at the end of time, the celebratory meal of which the poets sing and the prophets preach, the feast after God's work has at last come to its completion. Sabbath is a foretaste of that completion, an anticipation of the final chord in the unfolding divine symphony that has already been written—or better, of the celebratory, cosmic applause after that final chord.

And yet: precisely because it is a "foretaste," precisely because it is only one day out of seven, precisely because each week the Sabbath day comes to an end—the practice of observing the Sabbath points to how there is still work to do. The symphony may be written, but it is still unfolding, and we

---

2. Compare Partee, "Prayer as the Practice of Predestination," 254. Partee's case is that prayer is a practice by which disciples seek out and receive what God has preordained to do for them. If the Sabbath is conceived as a day of prayer and discernment, my argument and Partee's may be complementary.

have our part to play. This raises a second additional dimension of the Sabbath's "ceasing": in the version of the Ten Commandments in the book of Deuteronomy, the practice is explicitly tied to the story of the Israelites' exodus from enslavement (Deut 5:12–15). Because "you were a slave in the land of Egypt," and because God "brought you out from there with a mighty hand and an outstretched arm," so you, too, should in effect "release" yourself and your associates each week to observe the Sabbath, including all servants, domestic animals, and resident foreigners, so that all "may rest as well as you" (Deut 5:14). This latter phrase captures the Sabbath as a call to the work of equity and justice in society. Have you had a luxurious experience of the Day of Grace, a foretaste milk and honey, a glimpse of life "as if all your work, and God's work, is done"? Good! Now let it sharpen your appetite for a New Exodus, a new world in which all may enjoy that same milk and honey, indeed in which all may rest in joy and thanksgiving "as well as you." Roll up your sleeves, for there is much work to do—not in order to save you, but rather because you have been saved already, gracefully and powerfully, "with a mighty hand and an outstretched arm."

A third additional dimension of the Sabbath's "ceasing" is that its logic ramifies out across the Bible's library into an entire sabbatical structure, a broad poetic rhythm for human society as a whole. Every seventh day is a Sabbath day, and seven Sabbaths plus one span a "pentecost," a period of fifty days paradigmatic in both Judaism and Christianity. A year may be roughly divided into seven pentecosts; every seventh year is a Sabbatical Year, when even the land is given a rest and lies fallow; and seven sabbatical years plus one is a Jubilee Year, when slaves are freed and debts are forgiven (Exod 21, 23; Lev 25; Deut 15:12–18). The point here is not that all of these sevenfold protocols must be followed to the letter, or that they necessarily ever were followed historically, but rather that their underlying sabbatical spirit—including how the Sabbath and the doctrine of election mutually clarify each other—extends not just to our weekly schedules, but all the way out to the farthest reaches of the calendar, and of society as a whole. The logic of the Sabbath is the logic of election, and it is meant to pervade our lives and our life together.

Finally, a fourth additional dimension of the Sabbath is how it has evolved over time in Christian communities. For Christians, the Sabbath is Sunday, the day of resurrection, a day in which we stand, so to speak, "looking back" on God's saving work. Sunday looks back at Friday, the day Jesus declared, "It is finished" (John 19:30). The day of resurrection, then, retaliate. Precisely as such, Paul's turn toward "all Israel" sets the tone and the model for election's outward turn toward all of our neighbors, Jewish, Muslim, Hindu, or otherwise, on the principle of "if with the most difficult case, then also with all others." In other words, Paul's turn—or rather, Paul's exposition of God's turn—toward "all Israel" discloses part of the grammar of election: a turn outward toward others, and indeed not only toward "others" generically, but toward perceived "enemies" in particular. Our turn toward others, our being commissioned into the world, must emphatically include turning toward those with whom we have the most difficulty. For we may well find, Paul declares, that they are not "enemies" after all, at least not in the way we might think, but rather "enemies for your sake" (Rom 11:28). And in any case, they may well be among God's "beloved" and elect, notwithstanding how they may initially seem to differ from us.

Certain clannish Christian apologists may rush in at this point, insisting that Paul's testimony in Romans is that "all Israel" is saved "for the sake of their ancestors," as if God is a respecter of bloodlines—a principle quite foreign to Paul, the apostle to the Gentiles! But as we have seen, on the contrary, the essence of the apostle's case is the surprising, counterintuitive, provocative claim that God saves not only those who join the Jesus movement, but also those who expressly, pointedly refuse to do so. Suitably astounded, Paul breaks into ecstatic praise: "O the depth of the riches and wisdom and knowledge of God! How unsearchable are his judgments and how inscrutable his ways!" (Rom 11:33). The terms *unsearchable* and *inscrutable* are telling: God's grace, Paul insists, both overflows and overturns our expectations, defying all attempts to corral it within limits. For Paul, God's saving "all Israel" is no anomaly; rather, it is a characteristic, representative case study of a larger dynamic, an example of God's astonishing, surprising salvation—and a standing warning to anyone who would dare circumscribe the scope of God's mercy in advance. Strictly speaking, by the same token, Paul's doxology also signals that we cannot conclusively define salvation as universal any more than we can define it as partial, for salvation is God's business, not ours. God saves. We don't. But the unmistakable cutting edge of Paul's argument here, the insight that makes him break into praise, is that God's grace includes even those who seem to decline God's graceful invitation. The idea that this points toward an ultimately universal rescue of all humanity, and indeed of all creation, must remain theologically "hypothetical," even as the church humbly hopes for it, fervently prays for it, and faithfully, boldly expects it.

To paraphrase a line Martin Luther King, Jr. made famous, the arc of God's redemption is long, but it bends toward grace.[4]

And so we turn outward, commissioned into the world, sent to serve not only our friends, but also and especially our supposed "enemies." For they, too, may be among God's beloved and elect, whether or not they follow Jesus today, or will do so tomorrow. Our neighbors are God's children; they are among "all the families of the earth." And when we do encounter neighbors who are adversarial or indifferent to us or our convictions, how shall we relate to them? How shall we conceive them vis-à-vis the question of election? In a dazzlingly pluralistic world, richly religious and, in some quarters, increasingly nonreligious, the case of Christian relations with Jews can be a touchstone and a model that helps show us the way.

The church traditionally has not often understood itself in terms of its relation to God's ongoing covenant with the Jewish people. On the contrary, down through the centuries, many Christian authorities have proclaimed the church to be the true Israel, the faithful of all nations, in relation to which the actual people of Israel exist as a prefigure only, a foretaste, an anticipation of God's true covenant partner in the world.[5] Most of my life, this posture has been mine as well—and because I grew up with it, the theological horror at its heart took considerable time to rise to consciousness. To construe divine election in some other way than inclusive of Israel is profoundly mistaken, not least because it represents an egregious misreading of the Bible. I am now convinced that neither churches nor synagogues themselves fulfill Old Testament prophecies in a final sense. Scripture as a whole points beyond itself, toward God's future, a kingdom which—as Paul proclaims—Christians and Jews will inherit as brothers and sisters. With these broad strokes in mind, then, how should Christians conceive Jewish-Christian relations in the twenty-first century?

A first option—which we might call, "Christians First, Jews Second"—gained ground in the last century, thanks in particular to the Second Vatican Council. Based on Paul's work in Romans 9, this perspective calls Christians to turn toward their Jewish siblings with respect and gratitude for their remarkable witness through the ages to the God of heaven and

---

4. King's original line, which President Barack Obama so admired that he had it woven into the curved edge of a rug in the Oval Office, is a paraphrase likely drawn from abolitionist minister Theodore Parker's preaching. King put his version this way: "The arc of the moral universe is long, but it bends toward justice." King, "Remaining Awake," 223.

5. Wyschogrod, Abraham's Promise, 208.

earth; emphasizes the Jewishness of Jesus and most of his early followers; and affirms that both Jews and Christians are considered elect. Inside this election, however, there is a "first" and "second," an "A" and a "B"—and Christians occupy the "A" position. The theology of "replacement" is repudiated, but the idea of superiority persists. The ancient conversionist posture toward the Jews is softened, but maintained.

A second option—which we might call, "Jews First, Christians Second"—stands the first one on its head. On this view, Judaism is in the "A" position, as it has been since the first millennium BCE, and Paul is best interpreted as an apostle on a mission to open up the *Jewish* faith on behalf of a *Jewish* Savior. Israel remains God's chosen people, in relation to which God has done a long-promised "new thing" (Isa 43:19). Paul's startling message is that a new "B" has appeared to go with the old "A" in the form of a movement toward Israel's God by large numbers of people who are neither prepared nor required to become Jews. From the outset, after all, the election of Israel was so that "all the families of the earth shall be blessed" (Gen 12:3). Paul's pragmatism, his willingness to "become all things to all people, that I might by all means save some," implies that he envisioned a "people of God" of extraordinary spiritual range. In our new century, on this view, the question now facing Christ's church is how this range should be doctrinally described (1 Cor 9:22).[6]

This second option has much to recommend it, but a third is even more compelling, not least because it more fully embodies the spirit of mutuality and reciprocal respect prompted by the election doctrine itself. We may call this option a "Mutual Partnership" framework, since it sets aside entirely the idea of an "A" and a "B." The love of God elects human beings, and that love is deeper and more intimate than any ranking or pecking order would suggest. All haughtiness is ruled out. The full pattern of what Krister Stendahl calls "God's traffic plan" of redemption is ultimately a mystery to us, but the glimpse we get here in Romans confirms that the election of some need not imply the rejection of others.[7] Those cast down

---

6. On this "second option," see Wyschogrod, *Abraham's Promise*, 202–10; on Paul's attitude toward non-Christians, see Campbell, *The Deliverance of God*, 90–95; and on Paul's pragmatism, see Wall, "Acts of the Apostles," 191–249.

7. In place of the mistaken idea that Paul is proposing two different ways of salvation in Romans 8–12, one for Jews and one for Christians, Stendahl uses "God's traffic plan" as a more accurate image. Moreover, with regard to Christian humility, Stendahl writes that Paul ends his presentation on election in Romans "with reference to a mystery"—that is, the mystery that "all Israel will be saved"—"that makes the haughty and conceited

may later be lifted up, and those lifted up may be so lifted precisely for the sake of others, including those cast down. In this complex, mysterious choreography, no ranking of "A" and "B" is possible, and so Christians can only turn toward mutual partnership with Jews—a partnership, please note, that takes the form not merely of an occasional or limited "alliance," but rather of a whole way of life.[8]

For Christians, what would such partnership look like? With Jews, yes, but also with other religious people, as well as with people of no religion at all? The difference between partnership-as-alliance and partnership-as-way-of-life may be compared to the difference between a commercial association and a loving marriage. In the business world, practical and strategic considerations define both the nature and scope of a partnership. In marital companionship, however, each member seeks to love and be loved, to respect and be respected, befriend and be befriended, support and be supported. At its best, the key commitment in marriage is to keep this kind of love alive, nurturing it regularly. Likewise, the doctrine of election teaches companionable partnership as a way of life, like a marriage blessed by God to expand and distribute God's love for the world.

Can the Christian church, enlivened and shaped by a sound doctrine of election, be sent into the world in this quasi-conjugal spirit, turning outward toward our neighbors in ways that nurture reciprocal love and respect, manifesting mutual partnership as a way of life? We can indeed, God willing—and if Paul is any guide, the Holy Spirit's commission to do so is both clear and well underway. Marriage requires both deep humility and healthy self-assurance in order to turn outward, and as we have seen, these are precisely the benefits the doctrine of election can help provide. The practical virtues of a loving marriage—listening, respect, mercy, and service—should be the practical virtues of Christian life as a whole, acts carried out not in order to save ourselves or others, but rather out of joy and gratitude that God has already done the saving, and will continue to do so. For in the end, neither doctrine, religion, nor virtue will save us. God saves—and a revived conception of this central Christian idea can humble us, assure us, and draw us into deeper relationships and healthier communities, through which, we pray, God will bless the world with a mercy as wide as the sea.

---

thoughts of Christians toward the Jewish people to be just as ugly as they are." Stendahl, *Final Account*, 7.

8. Casal, "Partnership," 1.

Discussion Questions

Introduction

1. The best way to start a discussion is to begin where we are. Before reading *God Saves*, what opinions or impressions did you have, if any, regarding the doctrine of election or predestination? What questions do you have at the outset?

2. Boulton writes of various common objections to the doctrine of election. Have you heard any of these objections before, or found any of them compelling?

3. Titles are often revealing. What point is Boulton driving at by titling this book *God Saves*?

Chapter 1

1. When it comes to the scope of salvation, Boulton writes of a "remnant" view and a "universalist" view. What's the difference? And what third view does Boulton advocate? Which alternative makes most sense to you?

2. For Boulton, there is a "stain" on the history of the Christian doctrine of election. What is it, and what does it have to do with "replacement theology"?

3. What is the difference, for Boulton, between "ecstasy" and "en-stasy"?

4. What is the implicit doctrine of election underlying Cain's outlook and actions?

Chapter 2

1. What do you think Boulton has in mind when he writes, "Election is the doctrine that doctrine will not save us"?

2. For Boulton, what does it mean to call Jesus "the Elected One"? How does the transfiguration story illustrate this idea? And how do we participate in Jesus' election?

3. The doctrine of election is vividly portrayed, Boulton argues, in the rite of infant baptism. How so? Do you find this view persuasive?

4. According to Boulton, how is the election doctrine "apocalyptic"?

5. Boulton contends that Christianity has "interreligious DNA and direction" built into it. On what does he base this claim? Do you agree?

Chapter 3

1. According to Boulton, how is election a kind of commissioning?

2. What are the pros and cons of interpreting the struggles in our lives as a form of divine teaching or training? What are the pros and cons of rejecting this view?

3. Of the many "patriarchs" and "matriarchs" we meet in the book of Genesis, is any one in particular important to you? How so? Does Abraham stand out? And what about Joseph, the star of the musical *Joseph and the Amazing Technicolor Dreamcoat*? How do these ancient stories help clarify the mystery of election? And how does the doctrine of election help clarify the stories?

4. Has anything ever happened in your life in which, retrospectively, you can discern two levels of intention, reminiscent of Joseph's remark, "Even though you intended to do harm to me, God intended it for good" (Gen 50:20)?

5. Boulton argues that election's commissioning is virtually always a "commissioning to companionship" in the direction of some form of reconciliation. Do you agree? Why or why not?

Chapter 4

1. Boulton contends that the focus of election is not on the elect, but on God and the human relationship with God. How might stories from the book of Exodus illustrate this claim?

2. In contrast to the classic "Charlton Heston" version of Moses, Boulton argues that the exodus story actually portrays Moses, particularly at the story's beginning, as fundamentally insecure and in need of assurance. Do you agree? How does (or doesn't) the doctrine of election function to help assure us?

3. What practices—worship, Sabbath, holidays, and so on—do you experience as assuring and reassuring about God's love for you?

4. What does "efficacious grace" mean, and how does it encourage us to think about the relationship between human agency and divine agency?

Chapter 5

1. According to Boulton, what is the essence of the message of the Hebrew prophets? With this in mind, what does it mean to call the doctrine of election "prophetic"?

2. The world today is full of conflict inspired, or in any case supported, by religion. How might renewed attention to the doctrine of election make Christians less likely (or more likely) to contribute to such conflict?

3. Abraham Joshua Heschel contends that the prophets' "great contribution" was the discovery that a person "may be decent and sinister, pious and sinful." Do you agree with him that these apparently contrasting attributes can actually go together?

4. What does the prophet Hosea suggest about how we should understand election? In particular, what difference does it make that he casts the divine-human relationship in terms of love and marriage?

5. The story of the Last Judgment in Matthew 25 is one of the most well-known passages in the Bible. Do you see it the way Boulton does? What light does the story shine on election?

Chapter 6

1. In what way is the doctrine of election something a person thinks and believes? And in what way is it something she acts on and does?

2. For Paul, what is humanity's key problem (laid out in Romans 7), and what is the remedy (laid out in Romans 8)?

3. How does Paul arrive at the idea that "all Israel will be saved"—even those who do not follow Jesus? How does this exemplify what Boulton calls the doctrine of election's "turning outward"?

4. What does Boulton mean when he calls Christian faith and confession both "important" and "penultimate"?

5. Boulton argues that Paul's cry of praise—"O the depth of the riches and wisdom and knowledge of God!" (Rom 11:33)—is significant to the apostle's argument. How so?

Chapter 7

1. After reading about the Pope's visit to Bosnia, are you more hopeful about religion as a force for peace in the world? Why or why not?

2. Boulton contrasts Jesus' parable about where to sit at a banquet with the story of Cain and Abel. What does this contrast crystalize about what a sound doctrine of election looks like in practice?

3. What was Harriet Beecher Stowe's critique of the Westminster Confession? Do you agree with her? Why or why not?

Chapter 8

1. Is observing the Sabbath a part of your life? Why or why not? Can you imagine experiencing it as a taste of your salvation by the Electing God of love? How might Sabbath-keeping be a "practice of predestination"?

2. Boulton contends that worship, prayer, and the Lord's Supper can all be practices that deepen our understanding of election, and in turn, that the doctrine of election can help deepen our experiences of these practices. Do you agree? Why or why not?

3. Boulton interprets Paul's argument that "all Israel will be saved" as a rhetorical pattern or choreography that may apply to other groups as well. Is Israel's salvation a special, unique case? Or does it illustrate the idea that we should never claim to know the limits of God's mercy?

4. Boulton spells out three possible ways to understand the relationship between Christianity and Judaism when it comes to salvation: "Christians First, Jews Second," "Jews First, Christians Second," and "Mutual Partnership." What are the key differences between these options, and which one do you find most persuasive?

— *Appendix II* —

TULIP Today

THE ACRONYM TULIP SUMMARIZES five key principles of historic Reformed thought, with an emphasis on their implications for salvation. Proposed first as "Canons" at the Synod of Dort in the Netherlands (1618–1619) a half-century after Calvin's death, the five points provide us with a brief sketch of the Reformed faith. While in need of revision, TULIP illustrates nicely the theological challenges facing election doctrines today, highlighting issues of human responsibility and divine sovereignty as they relate to sin and redemption.

T: Total Depravity

At bottom, "total depravity" means that the effects of sin in human life are thoroughgoing, both at the level of the individual (i.e., there is no part or aspect of a human being which is exempt or immune from sin's distorting effects), and at the level of the community (i.e., there are no individuals or groups within humanity who are exempt or immune). Consequently, Christ comes for all because all have need of the salvation he brings. No one is in a position to earn or merit salvation. Everyone finds himself or herself living, as the prophet Isaiah puts it, "among a people of unclean lips" (Isa 6:5). As we'll see, the principles of total depravity and unconditional election go hand in hand.

U: Unconditional Election

Salvation comes from the other side, so to speak. It is never anything other than a miraculous *given*. It is not distributed according to any conditions or requirements; it is "unconditional." In Christian theology, it goes by the name of "grace." Indeed, the doctrine of election is an answer to the question of what grace entails. Genuine human freedom is never nullified in this mysterious process, though human merit, credit, and desert are decisively ruled out. From this angle, the starting point for one of the most common of religious worries—that others deserve salvation more than we do—evaporates. Redemption is both real and undeserved. As Paul puts it, God "chose us in Christ before the foundation of the world" (Eph 1:4).

L: Limited Atonement

In my view, the idea here—that the efficacy of God's saving work is limited to a subset of God's children—is profoundly mistaken, because the scope of salvation is manifestly beyond our ken. On the contrary, the gospel announcement about Christ's work in reconciling all things with God (that is, bringing all things into atonement or "at-one-ment") is distinctive precisely insofar as it specifies no limit known to us. We can only say, with the author of Colossians, that "Jesus is the image of the invisible God, the firstborn of all creation; for in him all things in heaven and on earth were created . . . through him God was pleased to reconcile to himself all things, whether on earth or in heaven, by making peace through the blood of his cross" (Col 1:15–16, 20).

Will God ultimately put limits on the efficacy or extent of Christ's work? Perhaps—and perhaps not. While some scriptural passages seem to suggest a mysterious limit, others seem to suggest an equally mysterious absence of any limit at all. Taken together, then, the mosaic of the Bible's witness pointedly leaves the question open, and so indirectly makes clear that we have no right to define the scope of God's salvation. When we do, we run the risk of ignoring God's call to humility (as Paul wisely puts it, "I will not boast, except of my weaknesses") and at the same time overlooking that grace is always for the lost, for the reprobate, for sinners: "God proves his love for us in that while we still were sinners, Christ died for us" (2 Cor 12:5; Rom 5:8). Indeed, if there is anything "limited" here, it is humankind's ability to discern, define, or declare the outer boundaries of God's redemptive work. Accordingly, if TULIP is to be preserved, the acronym's "L" should stand instead for "Limited Discernment" regarding salvation's scope, calling us both to humility and to the hope that, in the end, all shall be included in the circle of redemption.

I: Irresistible Grace

Human beings, come what may, are finally unable to reject or fall away from God's love, acceptance, and transformative grace. When God elects to save, God simultaneously grants to the rescued person or people the will and ability ultimately to accept that salvation. The grace that comes without preconditions (see the "U" above) also comes with the enabling conditions of its eventual acceptance, sooner or later (see the "P" below).

P: Perseverance of the Saints

Imagine a church building set on a piece of property beside a graveyard. The perseverance of the saints is best lifted up and discussed when "life is o'er, the battle done"—for example, at a Christian funeral. This idea is at once a testimony that the dearly departed have persevered, and a call to all living saints to take heart and follow their lead. But on an even deeper level, the idea strikes a note that both reflects and complements the irresistibility of grace. The perseverance of the saints speaks from the end of all things; it is a reassuring word that arrives, so to speak, from the future. In other words, what it means to be elect is to be "saved" definitively and permanently. Not one of the elect shall be lost. Divine love and faithfulness are steadfast, and God will not forsake God's children.

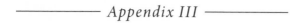

Suggestions for Further Reading

Sacvan Bercovich, *The American Jeremiad* (University of Wisconsin Press, 1978). This book is a "best book" on both election and preaching. A rhetorician and an American studies scholar, Bercovich has written a difficult, moving masterpiece. His grasp of the Christian pulpit is extraordinary.

G. C. Berkouwer, *A Half Century of Theology*, (Eerdmans, 1977). The Dutch Reformed theologian has also written a vibrant study of predestination itself: *Divine Election* (1960). But in this more accessible volume, Berkouwer summarizes the enormous energy surrounding the predestination doctrine discussion in twentieth-century Europe, and addresses the question of how seriously we can still say that election lies at the *cor ecclesia*, the heart of the church.

Shirley C. Guthrie, *Christian Doctrine*, 2d edition (Westminster John Knox, 1994). An accessible, readable volume by a beloved theology professor, with a fine chapter on election.

Christine Helmer, *Theology and the End of Doctrine* (Westminster John Knox, 2014). Using three champions of election from centuries past (Luther, Schleiermacher, and Barth), Helmer carefully redefines doctrine as more than simply a church teaching. On the contrary, she contends, doctrines are always and everywhere alive and open to change in a precise sense: they are socially constructed statements about the living God.

Abraham Joshua Heschel, *The Sabbath* (Farrar, Straus and Giroux, 1951/1979/2005). To re-grasp election today requires something on the order of a conversion. The heart of it for Christians is to encounter the tradition in which the Lord Jesus was raised. That tradition happens to be still alive and kicking, sitting beside us as a distinct and different "religion." How is that encounter to be arranged? Rabbi Heschel's classic is a wonderful place to start.

George Lindbeck, *The Nature of Doctrine* (Westminster John Knox, 1984/2009). Lindbeck's short and justly celebrated book is perhaps most remarkable for its robust expression of Christian doctrine's range in relation to theories of religion, to the encounter between Christianity and other religions, to the resolution of historic doctrinal conflict among Christian communities, and to the nature and task of theology.

Suzanne McDonald, *Re-Imaging Election* (Eerdmans, 2010). A powerful voice in the predestination discussion, McDonald's excitement about the election doctrine is striking and contagious. She argues convincingly that "representation" of God to others and of others to God is both a fertile and fitting answer to the question of election's purpose.

Jacob Neusner, *Judaism in the Beginning of Christianity* (Fortress, 1984). When Christianity first separated from its Jewish roots, how did things look from the other side? In brief compass, Jacob Neusner—the dean of Jewish religion scholars—provides a lucid summary.

Fleming Rutledge, *And God Spoke to Abraham: Preaching from the Old Testament* (Eerdmans, 2011). Reverend Rutledge is an Episcopal priest with a nationwide ministry of preaching and teaching. The Old Testament, she writes, is nothing less than the New Testament's "operating system." Readers interested in going further will gain much from her magnum opus: *Crucifixion* (2015).

Jonathan Sacks, *Not in God's Name: Confronting Religious Violence* (Shocken, 2015).While not entirely convincing in his treatment of the Apostle Paul, Rabbi Sacks has angels at his side in this beautiful summary of a life's work exposing the roots of religious violence, and indeed of violence more generally. A Jewish answer to what election is for.

Peter J. Thuesen, *Predestination: The American Career of a Contentious Doctrine* (Oxford University Press, 2009). This splendid historical volume leaves us in no doubt about the weight of predestination in American history, about its range well outside the Reformed tradition, and even about its continuing role in American life. If you have time to read only one book about our subject, this should be your choice.

William H. Willimon, *How Odd of God: Chosen for the Curious Vocation of Preaching* (Westminster John Knox, 2015). The most unusual offering on the list. Originally given as lectures at Princeton Seminary, Willimon's book is at once a spirited defense and an electric exposition of the election doctrine recast in the work of Swiss Reformed theologian Karl Barth.

Bibliography

Barth, Karl. *Church Dogmatics* II/2: *The Doctrine of God*. Translated by G. W. Bromiley. Edinburgh: T & T Clark, 1957.

Bellah, Robert N. *Religion in Human Evolution: From the Paleolithic to the Axial Age*. Cambridge, MA: Harvard University Press, 2011.

Berkouwer, G. C. *Divine Election*. Translated by Hugo Bekker. Grand Rapids: Eerdmans, 1960.

Bonhoeffer, Dietrich. *Christ the Center*. Translated by John Bowden. New York: Harper and Row, 1966/1978.

Book of Common Worship. Louisville: Westminster John Knox, 1993.

Boulton, Matthew Myer. *God Against Religion: Rethinking Christian Theology through Worship*. Grand Rapids: Eerdmans, 2008.

———. *Life in God: John Calvin, Practical Formation, and the Future of Protestant Theology*. Grand Rapids: Eerdmans, 2011.

Book of Common Worship: Pastoral Edition. Louisville: Westminster John Knox, 1993.

Brueggemann, Walter. "Exodus." In *The New Interpreter's Bible*, vol. I, 675–981. Nashville: Abingdon, 1994.

Campbell, Douglas A. *The Deliverance of God: An Apocalyptic Rereading of Justification in Paul*. Grand Rapids: Eerdmans, 2009.

Casal, Jose Luis. "Partnership as a 'Way of Life' for the Church." *Mission Crossroads* (Summer 2018) 1.

Crisp, Oliver D. *Deviant Calvinism: Broadening Reformed Theology*. Minneapolis: Fortress, 2014.

The Documents of Vatican II. New York: The America, 1966.

Edwards, Jonathan. *Writings on the Trinity, Grace and Faith*. Edited by Sang Hyung Lee. New Haven, CT: Yale University Press, 2003.

Gonzalez, Justo L. *A Brief History of Sunday*. Grand Rapids: Eerdmans, 2017.

Gottwald, Norman. *The Tribes of Yahweh*. Maryknoll, NY: Orbis, 1979.

Greenway, William. *For the Love of All Creatures: The Story of Grace in Genesis*. Grand Rapids: Eerdmans, 2015.

Hall, Douglas John. *The Cross in Our Context: Jesus and the Suffering World*. Minneapolis: Fortress, 2003.

———. *Thinking the Faith: Christian Theology in a North American Context*. Minneapolis: Augsburg Fortress, 1989/1991.

Heschel, Abraham Joshua. *The Prophets*. Part 2. New York: Harper and Row, 1962/1975.
———. *The Sabbath: Its Meaning for Modern Man*. New York: Farrar, Straus and Giroux, 1951.
King, Martin Luther, Jr. "Remaining Awake Through a Great Revolution." In *A Knock at Midnight: Inspiration from the Great Sermons of Reverend Martin Luther King, Jr.*, edited by Clayborne Carson and Peter Holloran, 201–24. New York: Warner, 2000.
Levenson, Jon. *Sinai and Zion: An Entry into the Hebrew Bible*. San Francisco: Harper Collins, 1985.
Lyman, Rick. "Pope Urges a Divided Bosnia to Heal." *The New York Times*, June 7, 2015.
MacCulloch, Diarmaid. *The Reformation: A History*. New York: Penguin, 2003.
McDonald, Suzanne. *Re-Imaging Election: Divine Election as Representing God to Others and Others to God*. Grand Rapids: Eerdmans, 2010.
The New Century Hymnal. Cleveland: Pilgrim, 1995.
Niebuhr, Reinhold. *The Nature and Destiny of Man*. Vol. II. New York: Scribners, 1943.
Partee, Charles. "Prayer as the Practice of Predestination." In *Calvinus Servus Christi*, edited by Wilhelm H. Neuser, 245–56. Budapest: Pressabteilung des Raday-Kollegiums, 1988.
Pelikan, Jaroslav. *The Christian Tradition: A History of the Development of Doctrine. Volume 5: Christian Doctrine and Modern Culture*. Chicago: University of Chicago Press, 1989.
———. *The Christian Tradition: A History of the Development of Doctrine, Volume 2: The Spirit of Eastern Christendom (600–1700)*. London: University of Chicago Press, 1974.
Siedentop, Larry. *Inventing the Individual: The Origins of Western Liberalism*. Cambridge MA: Belknap Press of Harvard University Press, 2014.
Small, Joseph D. *To Be Reformed: Living the Tradition*. Louisville: Witherspoon, 2010.
Sproul, R. C. *Chosen By God*. Carol Stream, IL: Tyndale, 1986/2010.
Stendahl, Krister. *Final Account: Paul's Letter to the Romans*. Minneapolis: Fortress, 1993/1995.
Taylor, Barbara Brown. *Leaving Church*. San Francisco: HarperOne, 2007.
Thuesen, Peter. *Predestination: The American Career of a Contentious Doctrine*. New York: Oxford University Press, 2009.
Tillich, Paul. "Moralisms and Morality: Theonomous Ethics." In *Theology of Culture*, 133–45. Oxford: Oxford University Press, 1959.
———. *Systematic Theology*. Vol. I. Chicago: University of Chicago Press, 1951.
Volf, Miroslav. *Free of Charge: Giving and Forgiving in a Culture Stripped of Grace*. Grand Rapids: Zondervan, 2005.
Wall, Robert W. "The Acts of the Apostles." In *The New Interpreter's Bible Commentary, Volume IX*, 1–292. Nashville: Abingdon, 2015.
"The Westminster Confession of Faith." *The Constitution of the Presbyterian Church (U.S.A.), Part I: Book of Confessions*. Louisville: OGA, 2002.
Wright, N. T. "Romans." In *The New Interpreter's Bible Commentary, Volume IX*, 317–664. Nashville: Abingdon, 2015.
Wyschogrod, Michael. *Abraham's Promise: Judaism and Jewish-Christian Relations*. Grand Rapids: Eerdmans, 2004.

Subject Index

Author Index

Scripture Index

Made in the USA
Middletown, DE
12 July 2022